FEARLESS AT WORK

FEARLESS AT WORK

Timeless Teachings for Awakening
Confidence, Resilience, and Creativity
in the Face of Life's Demands

MICHAEL CARROLL

Shambhala
Boston & London
2012

Shambhala Publications, Inc.
Horticultural Hall
300 Massachusetts Avenue
Boston, Massachusetts 02115
www.shambhala.com

9 8 7 6 5 4 3 2 1

First Edition

Printed in the United States of America

❀ This edition is printed on acid-free paper that meets the American National Standards Institute Z39.48 Standard.
♻ This book is printed on 30% postconsumer recycled paper. For more information please visit www.shambhala.com.
Distributed in the United States by Random House, Inc., and in Canada by Random House of Canada Ltd

Library of Congress Cataloging-in-Publication Data

Carroll, Michael.
Fearless at work: timeless teachings for awakening confidence, resilience, and creativity in the face of life's demands / Michael Carroll.
p. cm.
Includes bibliographical references.
ISBN 978-1-59030-914-8 (pbk.: alk. paper) 1. Self-confidence.
2. Resilience (Personality trait) 3. Creative ability. I. Title.
BF575.S39C37 2012
294.3'444—dc23
2012009629

CONTENTS

CONTENTS

PART THREE
Taming the Mind

PART FOUR
Establishing a Fearless Presence

PART FIVE
Living a Skillful Life

APPENDICES

FEARLESS AT WORK

INTRODUCTION

Rediscovering our
natural confidence

BEFORE WE BEGIN, I would like to invite you to take a short survey. In fact, the survey has only one question, so it won't take very long. In my role as a business consultant and executive coach, I often ask my clients to complete this single-item questionnaire, and I will ask you to do the same. *Remember:* there are no wrong answers, so trust yourself!

Confidential: **Official Workplace Survey**[*]

Instructions: Complete the following sentence with the
**very first word** that comes to mind

1. At work, I want to be _____ .

[*]© survey developed by AAW Associates—all rights reserved

While no scientist has vetted my Official Workplace Survey as statistically reliable, I can report that there are some patterns to the responses, and here are the six most frequent answers to date:

Happy
Successful
Stress-free
Effective
Fulfilled
Appreciated

Sound familiar? Needless to say, such aspirations come as no surprise. Given the demands and relentless pace of our modern-day workplace, it is little wonder that most of us would like a little stress-free happiness on occasion. Success and fulfillment? A little appreciation for a job well done? Isn't that what we are all looking for at work?

After forty-five years of making a living and thirty-seven years of Buddhist training, I'm not so sure. My survey indicates that most of us think we want to be happy, successful, and stress-free at work, but we also know that such aspirations are wishful thinking. We all know that work offers both success and failure, happiness and angst. We know that work, indeed all of life, unavoidably presents both rewards and penalties, joys and disappointments. So, while most of us may wish to be happy and successful at work, what we really want, if we bring our aspirations down to earth, is to be *confident:* confident that no matter what work offers up—success or failure, happiness or disappointment, recognition or indifference—we can unshakably rely on ourselves to be self-assured, resourceful, and at our ease.

But somehow, for so many of us, such workplace confidence seems elusive, and instead of feeling resourceful and resilient, we too often find ourselves *hoping* for success, *chasing* happiness, *craving* rewards, and *fearing* the worst.

In 1998, after ten years of working for a major publishing firm, I was laid off. Our company had been acquired, and I, along with many other executives, was displaced and invited to leave. For the most part, we were all treated well in our departure, and I, for one, left with few hard feelings. Yet I was worried about my future prospects.

On my final day I spent my time saying farewell to some close colleagues, and I recall a particularly insightful conversation with a division president, Sharon, which to this day reminds me to step past my aspirations and, instead, confidently wake up to my life.

After spending several minutes reminiscing, I began to wrap up our conversation and, with a shake of hands, turned to leave Sharon's office when she said, "Michael, what's the matter?"

I turned and paused before dutifully responding, "What's the matter? What do you mean 'what's the matter'? I lost my job!"

And she gently asked, "So what's the worst that could happen?"

"What's the worst that could happen?" I responded with a bit of panic in my raised voice. "I could lose my home, my savings, and be out on the street with my family. That's what could happen," I pleaded.

Without a moment's hesitation and with a tone of surprise in her voice, Sharon responded, "And you couldn't handle that?"

I was dumbfounded by her response and I felt embarrassed. Clearly my colleague had seen something in me that I had lost touch with. And what she so wisely observed was how my fear had blinded me: in the midst of the confusion and bewilderment of losing a job, I had also lost touch with myself.

My colleague was right, of course. I adapted and moved successfully in a new direction. But the real challenge for me—and for many of us in such circumstances—is not about charting a new course, becoming successful again, or avoiding disaster. In many respects that is the easy part. The true challenge for all of us in facing life's difficulties is about stepping past our panic and trusting our noble instincts: *it's about rediscovering our natural fearlessness.*

Being fearless when losing a job or when facing any of life's challenges is not about learning to defend ourselves. Nor is it a matter of having a "stiff upper lip" where we try to convince ourselves that we can shoulder any burden and withstand any insult. Such confidence, while admirable, in the end is just hoping for the best. Nor is fearlessness a form of aggression, where we attack our world out of bravado, flexing our emotional muscles, seeking to conquer life's challenges. More often than not, such aggression is toxic and arrogant—a kind of energetic cowardice masquerading as toughness.

The kind of confidence that remains fearlessly unshaken in the face of life's often terrifying paradoxes—instinctively resourceful and at ease—is not something we can manufacture.

Such fearlessness is our birthright; it is what makes us human at our most fundamental level.

This book is about rediscovering the fearlessness that defines us as noble human beings.

In many respects, we are all quite familiar with fearlessness. A teenager singing opera, a mother loving her dying son, a gymnast executing somersaults, a young soldier sacrificing her life, a poet reading aloud—acts large and small, all intimate and brave and utterly human. Such fearlessness is quite recognizable and inspiring. Yet personally connecting with this fearlessness is one of life's most demanding challenges, and there are many outstanding traditions that we can look to for guidance: the vision quest of the Lakota Sioux, the martial disciplines of aikido, the humanitarian practices of some health organizations, even the rigors of a modern-day athletic regime. While each and every human being is intimately familiar with being fearless, we often need help expressing such confidence, and we are fortunate to have many diverse traditions to support our efforts.

Over the past thirty-seven years, it is my good fortune to have been trained by several kind and wise Buddhist teachers in contemplative disciplines for cultivating fearlessness, and this book offers contemplations, practices, and principles drawn from these traditions:

- Kagyu-Nyingma meditative disciplines
- Shambhala Warrior practices

- Sun Tzu's military principles
- Kasung-command protection methods

For me personally, it is a rare joy and honor to be counted among the millions of people from over dozens of generations to have followed these traditions in order to live a decent and courageous life. For those who would like to learn more about these traditions of fearlessness, see appendix D.

Bringing these four traditions and their contemplative practices vividly into our lives is not just about work, of course, and the scope of *Fearless at Work* is broader than just making a living. Engaging our lives confidently, by definition, must extend well beyond the job to include many rich and penetrating human moments, such as sitting quietly by the bedside of a dying friend, falling in love for the first time, or just learning to walk. In the end, this book is as much about being confident in life as it is about being *fearless at work*.

While a contemplative practice in its own right, this book also builds on many of the principles offered in my two prior books, *Awake at Work* and *The Mindful Leader*. For example, the slogan "First to pacify, last to destroy" from *Awake at Work* generally explains how the four-armed mahakala protection principles can be applied on the job.[1] In the present volume such principles are greatly expanded on and woven throughout many of the suggested contemplations. Similarly, in the case of *The Mindful Leader*, the principle of vulnerability, for example, is presented as the primary leadership gesture for inspiring the best in others. Here, in this volume, such openness is more fiercely revealed as formidable and tough, placing even greater demands on those of us wishing to live a fearlessly awake life. On occasion, I have footnoted references to *Awake at Work* and *The Mindful Leader* for those who wish to tie the three volumes together as a unified practice.

Finally, *Fearless at Work* is based on making a simple, practical gesture: *sitting down and being still.* Much more on this topic will be covered throughout the book, but it is vital at the very beginning to emphasize this basic point: in order to step past our fear, see life clearly, and live nobly and confidently, we will need to tame our minds—we will need to look carefully at our restless panic and learn to let go, open, and relax. And while some of us may choose different paths—paths that are fitting and inspiring, no doubt— here, taming the mind is about learning to *sit down and be still,* an easy gesture but one that is exquisitely demanding.

How to Use This Book

In order to begin, a few pointers will help on how to use this book.

Fearless at Work is organized as a contemplative practice of thirty-eight slogans designed to provide pithy instructions for enlivening fearlessness on the spot in everyday life. This contemplative tradition of slogan practice goes back many centuries in Tibet and is best exemplified by the one-thousand-year-old Tibetan Buddhist teaching called *The Root Text of the Seven Points of Training the Mind,* or *lojong,* by the renowned Bengali Buddhist master Atisa Dipamkara Srijnana.[2] The lojong practice organized Atisa's oral teachings into fifty-nine memorable slogans, shorthand instructions for cultivating compassion and wakefulness, and the practice has been widely used throughout Tibet and today throughout the world.

Inspired by this tradition, the slogans in this book encourage the practitioner to read, contemplate, and comment on the thirty-eight slogans repeatedly so that the slogans can be easily recalled throughout the day, spontaneously providing guidance. By keeping alert to the slogans in this way, daily events begin to unfold as a form of contemplative practice wherein the slogans' natural wisdom reveals ordinary experiences to be extraordinary opportunities to live life fearlessly.

While slogan practice is a gradual, unfolding path, it can also be provocative and at times penetrating, sharply waking us up to reality and inviting us to question many of the preconceptions that we have about our lives. I encourage you to read and contemplate the slogans at your own pace, engaging the themes and ideas and testing them against your own experience.

The practice is organized into five sections:

1. The five primary slogans
2. Exploring the ironies of cowardice
3. Taming the mind
4. Establishing a fearless presence
5. Living a skillful life

Part one, "The Five Primary Slogans," introduces us to the spiritual facts of life, so to speak. Here we lay the ground for all thirty-eight slogans, define our terms, and make sure we are all on the same page. In this section we are asked to acknowledge that life can be and often is remarkably painful, lonely, unpredictable, and distressing. Yet if we have the courage to be honest with ourselves, we must also recognize that life is also profoundly and relentlessly delightful. Learning to accept, perhaps even celebrate, such a paradox introduces the possibility of living a fearlessly abundant life with extraordinary command over our circumstances.

In part two, "Exploring the Ironies of Cowardice," we come face-to-face with having to admit that we are cowards. Here we recognize the unsettling dilemma that in order to be fearless, we have to admit that we are, in fact, afraid—which, paradoxically, is a gesture of courage itself. Throughout this section we explore and contemplate the ironies of being a coward: the more we try to hide, the more exposed we appear; the more we try to secure ourselves, the more we author a threatening life; and so on. By contemplating the pointlessness of cowardice, we gradually exhaust our fascination with false hopes and exaggerated fears and begin to consider the possibility of living a fearless life.

Part three, "Taming the Mind," offers a kind of extended instruction in mindfulness-awareness meditation. Taken in sequence, each slogan builds on the ones before it, illustrating how mindfulness-awareness tames the restless mind, opens us to the present moment, reveals our natural fearlessness, and promotes a sane and confident life.

In part four, "Establishing a Fearless Presence," we explore the emotional stance we take when we live life fearlessly. Instead of crouching defensively, indulging the insincere emotions of a coward, in this section we contemplate the possibility of standing up straight, where we recognize our broken heart as wise, our fear as an invitation, and our aloneness as romantic and strong. Being willing to savor our rich and raw emotions directly without sugar-coating them or dumbing them down, we discover our feelings to be bodily wisdom—alert, powerful, and insightful.

In part five, "Living a Skillful Life," we discover that living fearlessly puts us into a spiritual conversation with a world that is willing to teach us how to be skillful. In the past, we may have preferred the language of control with the syntax of emotional scorecards, exaggerated pleasures, and low-grade anxiety. And not surprisingly, such a cowardly dialogue with life left us deaf, dumb, and blind to the wisdom around us. Here we explore the language of confidence—a language our world understands and responds to—and we become familiar with the primordial wakefulness of life where the energy is intense, vast, and evanescent, fraught with spiritual meaning that is at once awesome and unspeakable, yet gone and traceless the very moment it arises. By letting go of our panic, opening to this moment with no guarantees, and relaxing, we meet our world as teacher, friend, and guide and we learn to live a skillful life.

While you may prefer to read these five sections of *Fearless at Work* through from beginning to end, the book is primarily designed to be applied as a contemplative discipline, combined with a regular mindfulness-awareness meditation practice. For those who wish to use the book for contemplation, here are a few suggestions.

Study the Five Primary Slogans First

There are five fundamental reminders that form the basis of the contemplation practice:

1. Face the fierce facts of life
2. No delight; no courage
3. Recognize fear
4. Discover the jewel of fearless abundance
5. Command gracefully

Before you consider the other thirty-three slogans, I highly recommend that you read and reflect on these five first.

Randomly Select Slogans

Once you have familiarized yourself with the five primary slogans, I suggest you randomly select other slogans to contemplate. You do not have to read all the slogans in order, one after another. You may choose to glance over the table of contents and select a slogan that seems to be speaking to you, or you can simply open the book randomly and begin reading the slogan that you find there. After finishing a slogan, take a brief moment to set the book aside and simply reflect on what you've read.

Watch How the Slogans Spontaneously Arise

In the course of your job and everyday life, events will most likely trigger your recalling a slogan. When that occurs, be highly attentive—permit your natural curiosity to engage the situation as it unfolds.

For example, let's consider the slogan "No delight; no courage," which recounts an old Taoist tale of a young boy facing impending death in the jaws of a tiger. Let's suppose that you have taken some time to read and contemplate the slogan, and as the tale suggests, have reflected on how fear can, at times, blind us to life's many delights and how living courageously requires that we appreciate simple joys. Now, one day you are home but very concerned about a work project that is derailing. You have been e-mailing and phoning your colleagues, and the distress among the team has you on edge and a bit panicky. As you are frantically responding to an e-mail, your cat, Georgio, leaps onto your desk with a note tied around his neck that reads, "Hey, Dad, wanna play?" and you turn to see your seven-year-old daughter peeking around the corner with her soccer ball in hand. And right there you recall the slogan "No delight; no courage," and you recognize that savoring such delight requires the courage to let go of the worry, stress, and fear and to fully and fearlessly taste life.

By permitting the slogan *no* "No delight; no courage," to blend with our experience of our daughter and our stressful livelihood *as we experience our daughter and stressful livelihood,* we experience "contemplation in action." This has to do with experimenting with the new perspective the slogan provokes, permitting our attitude to shift, viewing our life and our work from a new angle, and becoming familiar with our natural confidence.

Deliberately Contemplate the Slogans

You can also try contemplating and recalling the slogans more deliberately by rereading, discussing, and commenting on them. A five-step instruction for contemplating the slogans is outlined in the back of the book (appendix E). Here are some other ideas for working with the slogans:

- Each morning, select a slogan for the day. Read it before beginning work, then look for ways to apply that slogan on the job.
- Conclude sitting-meditation sessions by reading and contemplating a selected slogan.
- Keep a journal of your experiences and reflections about the slogans.
- Write a slogan on your daily calendar, where it will catch your eye throughout the day.
- Copy the slogans onto index cards and place a selected slogan discreetly on your desk by your computer or near the phone as a way to have ongoing access to the slogan's guidance.
- Memorize all thirty-eight so that you can more easily recall them at will.

Finally, *Fearless at Work* is not a manual for "solving fear" or a map for living a fear-free life. Rather, this book is about living life fearlessly—agile, noble, and open to all experience (success and failure, happiness and grief, insult and praise, pleasure and pain)—with delight and courage. Drawing on thousands of years of teachings and millions of people's experience, this book seeks to make a modest contribution, to lend a helping hand to a world that is too often afraid to help itself. And in the words of my teacher, Chögyam Trungpa,

When we are afraid of ourselves and afraid of the seeming threats the world presents, then we become extremely selfish. We want to build a little nest, our own cocoons, so that we can live our lives in a secure way. But we can be much more brave than that. . . . We must try to think how we can help this world. If we don't help, nobody will. It is our turn to help the world.[3]

PART ONE

THE FIVE PRIMARY SLOGANS

"Remembering that I'll be dead soon is the most important tool I've ever encountered to help me make the big choices in life. Because almost everything—all external expectations, all pride, all fear of embarrassment or failure—these things just fall away in the face of death, leaving only what is truly important. Remembering that you are going to die is the best way I know to avoid the trap of thinking you have something to lose. You are already naked. There is no reason not to follow your heart."

—Steve Jobs, cofounder and former CEO, Apple Inc. (1955–2011)

The five slogans in this section are the root of the practice, offering core guidance for expressing our natural confidence in everyday life:

1. Face the fierce facts of life
2. No delight; no courage
3. Recognize fear

4. Discover the jewel of fearless abundance
5. Command gracefully

When we permit these slogans to inform our daily life, we learn to engage our experience on its terms, not ours, stepping past our hesitation to fully savor life's fierceness and delights. And by training in the practice of mindfulness-awareness meditation, we discover we are fearlessly abundant: free, confident, and skillful.

1

Face the fierce facts of life

To LIVE A FEARLESS, confident life and resolve the challenge of cowardice, we must examine the distressing side of our experience: we must "face the fierce facts of life."

To be human hurts—at times unbearably so.
Anything can and does happen.
Each of us is alone: we are born alone and we die alone.
No one and nothing can save us from our lives.
We are going to die—very soon.
And when we die, 99.99 percent of the world won't notice.
And those who do notice will forget . . . often.

To Be Human Hurts—at Times Unbearably So

In one sense, such a simple statement may seem a bit ludicrous. We all stub our toes; we all taste life's stark tragedies; who doesn't get a C on occasion when we expect an easy A? Yet, if we examine our approach to life's ordeals honestly, we will notice a telling hypocrisy: *we often view life's problems as unjust impositions rather than simple facts of life.* In too many circumstances, it isn't that "life hurts" but more pathetically "why me?" So, in order to remove any doubt about the fact that to be human hurts, let's consider a few potent details:

- About thirteen people die from cancer every second worldwide, and the number is expected to exceed twenty-two people per second by 2030.[1]
- Of American adults surveyed, 59 percent believe that dropping the nuclear bomb on Hiroshima and Nagasaki was a good idea.[2]
- On any typical day, the planet loses forty to one hundred species.[3]
- According to UNICEF, twenty-four thousand children die each day due to poverty. And they "die quietly in some of the poorest villages on earth, far removed from the scrutiny and the conscience of the world. Being meek and weak in life, these dying multitudes are even more invisible in death."[4]
- Over 180 million people died in all the wars, massacres, slaughters, and oppressions of the twentieth century—far more than any century in history.[5]

Anything Can and Does Happen

There are an infinite number of additional statistics and stories that could further illustrate the fierce fact that life is painful. And while many of us in the economically developed world have countless toys and distractions that appear to shield us from these facts, the reality is that such suffering can and does happen to all of us all the time. No matter who or where you are, life can serve up just about any ordeal whenever it is inclined to do so. In short, just about anything can and does happen to us.

Each of Us Is Alone: We Are Born Alone and We Die Alone

All of us have some friends, loved ones, and colleagues—just a glance around reveals that we share our lives with many others. And in today's global economy, we are more intimately connected to our neighbors around the world than ever before. Yet, despite our many relationships, we have to go it alone in the end, in very basic, immediate terms. Pause for a moment and consider all those whom you have loved or known in your life. Where are they right now? Are they even thinking of you? And when you go to bed tonight, even if you are with your best friend and loved one, you will close your eyes alone.

No One and Nothing Can Save Us from Our Lives

Being raised a Christian, I was expected to behave myself and in return I would be "saved" from life's disappointments—at death, of course—though to be fair, many Christians prefer being "saved" while alive. And in business, there is the widespread feeling that by accumulating enough wealth, we can protect ourselves from life's difficulties—a kind of being saved materialistically. Or, for many, falling in love, getting married to the "love of my life," can appear to be a ticket to safety. Drugs, gods, gurus, love, or money—all seem to be full of promise. But, alas, none can rescue us from reality. There is no way in and no way out.

We Are Going to Die—Very Soon

One hundred and fifteen of us die every second, mostly from diseases such as heart ailments, infections, and strokes. And while some of us may live to a ripe old age, it does appear that most of us experience death as arriving suddenly and without warning—*even when all indications are that we are about to die.* The suggestion here is that by examining carefully right here, right now, we will notice that all indications are that we are, in fact, about to die. The moment is not far off at all.

And When We Die, 99.99 Percent of the World Won't Notice

Of the 115 people who just died this very second, how many do you know? Unless we happen to be Theodore Roosevelt or Mother Teresa, the chances are that when we die, no one, relatively speaking, will notice.

And Those Who Do Notice Will Forget . . . Often

Two people I loved tremendously, my mother and father, both died. Their deaths broke my heart. Today I think of them on occasion—sometimes cheerfully, sometimes with deep sadness.

Most of the time, I don't think of them at all. But I do live my life as decently as possible in their memory.

In the end, by facing the fierce facts of life, we must acknowledge that our very existence is startling: both astounding and terrifying all at once. We can pull back full of fear, cowering and denying, or step right in fearlessly, clear-eyed and confident. It's a choice we will make moment by moment for the rest of our lives.

2

No delight; no courage

ONE OF MY FAVORITE Taoist stories passed down through the centuries recounts the tale of a young boy caught in a most distressing predicament, where fearlessness is not a matter of braving untold challenges or shouldering heavy burdens but about taking delight in the midst of life's inevitable demands.

One afternoon, like many afternoons before, a young boy, Simha, walked along the edge of the jungle on his way home from work. This day, however, he noticed that he was being stalked by a tiger, who, remaining concealed in the shadows and tall grass, was silently angling to ambush him at an approaching narrow point in the path.

Being a clever boy and not wanting to be a meal for the tiger, Simha slowly changed direction and then, without warning, quickly sprinted for a nearby abandoned stone quarry where he felt sure he would find refuge if he could outrun the shadowing tiger.

And sure enough, when Simha reached the quarry he rushed toward the towering stone wall and, grabbing hold of a vine that had grown down the cliff, pulled himself up off the ground and safely out of the reach of the tiger, who arrived seconds too late to grab him. To his relief, the tiger roared and jumped but could not reach him as he, hand over hand, climbed the vine toward the top.

As Simha climbed closer to his escape at the top of the cliff, he suddenly noticed that a second tiger—a tiger that he had not spotted earlier—had maneuvered to the top of the cliff and was stationed patiently at the other end of the vine, also awaiting Simha as a meal. Below, he could see a tiger pacing and growling; above, he could see another licking its chops.

As he paused to reflect on his distressing circumstances, Simha glimpsed a pair of mice playing among the vines and greenery. One was black, the other white, and as they went about their business they would occasionally stop and nibble at the vine that suspended Simha along the face of the cliff and between the two tigers. Each nibble frayed the vine further and Simha's predicament grew more and more precarious.

Then, glancing off to his left, Simha noticed a dazzling-red, perfectly ripe strawberry nestled among the foliage. And for a moment he paused and wondered at such a marvel, stretching out to pick the berry that was ever so slightly out of his reach. Then, shifting his weight, he swung the vine back and forth until he could snatch the strawberry from its nest. He held the fully ripe red fruit in his hand, smiled, and took a full bite. And true to its appearance, the strawberry was delicious beyond compare—an occasion of radiant, flavorful delight.

Now, as with most stories where we are literally left hanging, we may ask ourselves, "What happens next? Does Simha escape? Does he toss those pesky mice off the cliff? How does he outsmart the tigers?" But in this case, there are no resolutions to these questions, because it isn't in the resolution but in the taste of the strawberry that we learn the lesson of Simha's story.

In many respects, Simha's circumstances reflect where we all find ourselves as human beings. The tiger of death is ever present, at times unseen, but always getting closer. And like Simha, we may cleverly seek to avoid its grasp, but in the end must acknowledge the presence of the tiger—the persistent reality of death.

Now, the presence of a tiger can focus our attention, waking us up to some ironies, the black and white mice that fritter away our hold on our lives: hope and fear, praise and blame, success and failure. But using such dualities to keep score seems oddly pointless in such circumstances—dangling from a cliff in the presence of death's tigers. Young or old, rich or poor, successful or struggling, healthy or infirm, the tiger awaits all equally, despite the score.

But, in the midst of what for so many of us would be desperate, dismal circumstances, Simha notices, then delights in, a simple gesture: the tasting of a berry. And it is here that we discover a formidable truth about living a fearless life.

To be human is to confront truly difficult circumstances, no doubt: disease, poverty, tragedies, and frustrations of all kinds. Yet, for all of us, there is always, *always* the possibility of delight:

to awaken to life's rich, sensual wonders such as sipping a glass of water, glimpsing the vast sky, touching another's face, or simply having a nose. Appreciating our lives naturally, almost effortlessly, in this way, right in the midst of life's tigers and mice, requires us to bravely acknowledge something powerful about our human dilemma, something that is red, dazzling, and fully ripe. Maybe right within our grasp is this vividly ripe moment, wonderfully delightful, if only we have the daring to simply recognize it.

The slogan "No delight; no courage" reminds us that the fierce facts of life are unavoidable but not the entire story, because to live a fearless life requires that we taste life fully. And what Simha realizes in tasting that berry—and what we all can realize in our lives—goes well beyond just counting our blessings in the midst of life's predicaments. It is about accepting an invitation to be delightfully human, moment by moment, for the rest of our lives.

3

Recognize fear

IN ORDER TO REDISCOVER our natural confidence and live a fearless life, we must examine the challenge: we must "recognize fear."

We can take various perspectives on such a topic. Anthropologists trace fear back millions of years to our days as small mammals bumbling beneath jungle shrubs at the feet of massive carnivores. Fear was our mechanism for sensing and reacting instinctively to dangers of all kinds. We would fight, fly, or freeze when facing a threat, and those of us who made the right choice got to live another day.

Or we could explore fear from the view of a neurophysiologist, examining our brain and nervous system. When confronted with a visual conflict as simple as a misplaced symbol or an unknown sound, parts of our brain light up that focus our attention and signal a need to problem solve. Fear, for the neurophysiologists, is a stimulus to investigate, discern, and resolve.

Or we could trace words to their origin, examining the etymology of *coward*, for example, where animals are made to crouch in terror, tails between their legs, lowering themselves and trading their nobility for subservience in order to gain safety.

Taking a Buddhist perspective on fear, however, requires that we make a simple, yet somewhat outrageous, observation: *fear does not exist.* This is not to say we don't experience fear and its many forms. Of course we are afraid of death and pain, afraid that we can't handle life. We fear new situations and the unknown. Yet, while we may want to define fear, explore fear, and possibly even resolve it, we first must acknowledge that we cannot actually find such a solid thing as "fear" at all. Like everything else in life, fear has no fixed point but is instead fluid, unpredictable, and livelier than either a word or a scientific study. So in order to explore such a thing, we will need to move with it, live it—"be" it, so to speak. Whether we are mildly anxious about an impending surgery or deeply distressed about losing our favorite pencil, sickened at the death of our child or utterly terrified by a raging war, fear is starkly intimate, woven into our lives, and shaping how we choose to spend the few hours we live on this planet.

In order to recognize fear, then, we will need to examine our experience, right here, right now. So let's pause for a moment and take stock of our situation.

On the one hand, circumstances seem pretty obvious. We are Mary or Bob. We have a job and family and friends. We have an address and we have a bedroom and a kitchen. We have a "biography"—we went to certain schools; we fell in love with various partners; we have pets and credit cards, coin collections, and favorite movies. And right now we are sitting somewhere as a particular body that has all kinds of lively little features—some that we enjoy, some that perturb us, and many that we take for granted.

On the other hand, when we examine this biography closer, what at first glance may appear to be obvious becomes elusive. Mary or Bob—these are just words that our parents were kind enough to offer us at our birth. We are not Mary or Bob. We are not our names.

Schools and friends, pets and credit cards—while they are very real at the moment, when we actually live our lives through them, now at this moment, right here, right now, they are mere memories. And our body—vivid and visceral—seems to function with or without our permission, as much an unknown as it is a familiarity.

When we pause and take stock of our experience at its most fundamental level, who we are is more elusive than certain, more ungraspable than apparent. The background of our lives, when brought into the foreground, reveals a sharp, all-pervading uncertainty. Nothing—not our name, not our biography or our history, friends, or relations—nothing is as certain as it seems.

Normally, we don't attend to this shapelessness. We go about our lives as Mary and Bob living our biography. But when the elusive, uncertain nature of life shifts from background to foreground, as it always does, we struggle and panic. Falling in love with a colleague, being diagnosed with cancer, or just missing an appointment, we instinctively sense that life happens in a way that we cannot grasp, and we become bewildered.

Becoming familiar with such bewilderment is how we examine and recognize fear. However, this is not a matter of analysis or therapy. We are not interested in explaining our reasons for being afraid or even resolving our anxiety. In this case, we want to see our fear directly, to touch it and recognize it, and we learn to do so by practicing mindfulness-awareness meditation.

One of the fascinating challenges in meditation, especially in the beginning of getting to know the practice, is how uncomfortable we are with doing nothing. We sit down on the cushion, gather our minds, and notice how restless, impatient, and anxious we are by simply sitting still. This experience may be annoying, but it is vital that we see this discomfort clearly, for it is here in being bewildered and panicky that we can learn to touch the shapeless uncertainty of life and recognize fear.

Sitting on the cushion minute by minute, hour after hour, week in, week out, at some point we discover that we are panicking because we are not sure what is going on. Experiencing this type of panic is like being dazed, disoriented, and in a kind of fog, asking ourselves over and over again, "What's going on here? Am I going to be OK? Is this working out?"[1]

In trying to get an answer to these questions and get a grasp on our uncertain circumstances, we breed cowardice with story lines of all kinds: "I'm freaked out because I am going to lose my job and won't be able to handle life!" or "I'm worried because Sasha is going to fall in love with Gerald and leave me behind!" or "I think my foot has cancer—it hasn't been behaving itself lately."

Through the practice of mindfulness-awareness meditation, however, we learn that we need not perpetuate panic and breed cowardice with all kinds of stories. Instead, we can experience the shapeless uncertainty without anything to hold on to. Placing our attention on our breath, we go out and "gap"—we are sitting in space, afraid, with no answers. We let go of our story lines and logics and leap into the uncertainty, completely groundless. We join our fear with the total uncertainty of it all.

Such groundlessness can be terrifying, no doubt. Being alive with no deals—no emotional security pacts, no assurances against life's tragedies, no numbing anesthesia from drugs or TV, no guarantees whatsoever—is tremendously exposing. Yet, when we are completely honest with ourselves, we discover not only that we are primordially exposed but that *panicking is optional.* Being exposed to life is sharply real and unavoidable, but being a coward is not required.

By having the courage to recognize fear and embrace the shapeless uncertainty of our experience over and over again, literally thousands of times on and off the cushion, the fog of our bewilderment gradually lifts, and we discover a most perplexing and delightful irony: *the uncertainty that has been bewildering us is, in fact, the very freedom that we have been looking for.* In our panic to grasp the ungraspable, to seek assurances where none are possible, and to find ground where none exists, we have blinded ourselves with cowardice and overlooked the fact that we have no need for assurances and that our groundlessness is delightfully awake and free.

The slogan "Recognize fear" encourages us to explore our panic, bewilderment, and anxiety straightforwardly through the practice of mindfulness-awareness meditation, where we can learn to acknowledge our fear and confidently touch life's uncertainty. Whether we are facing death or disappointment, surprise or shock, when we recognize fear, we recognize that we can leap into life's shapelessness without false assurances, cowardly logics, or anxious story lines. And by leaping in with no guarantees, we stop seeking a life free from fear, but instead discover how to live life fearlessly.

4

Discover the jewel of fearless abundance

IT'S FRIDAY AFTERNOON, and you are about to attend a meeting in thirty minutes that you have been quietly dreading for the past two months. Your boss has been convening for the last hour with the two senior project managers who oversee your work, and given the feedback you have been receiving lately, your role as the systems developer on the over-budget, late, and increasingly unappreciated billing system is in question. The past two weeks have been particularly frustrating, since those accountable for the project have suddenly donned "Teflon suits" and become overly "sympathetic" in appreciating "your" dilemma. In short, all indications are that you have been chosen to be the scapegoat for a project gone haywire, and those who should be shouldering the responsibility with you have been orchestrating a narrative to ensure that you receive the blame and they get to solve the problem—you.

As with all problems at work, there are many sides to the story, and you have yours. You have prepared your points and antici-pated your bosses' responses. You have your documents, e-mails, and memos outlining all the missteps that others made in devel-oping the billing system, and you are ready to defend yourself. But, at the same time, you are feeling defeated, angry, and mistreated, and you have been rehearsing these emotions and logics for months. It has been tiring, difficult, and lonely, and now you are about to endure the inevitable ritual of being fired.

Many of us have found ourselves in some version of this situa-tion: feeling under siege, unappreciated, and powerless in the face of sharp and excessive workplace demands. And while the circum-stances may vary, many of us, when confronted by such difficulties, experience a fear that can feel primal—a sense of profound inad-equacy and isolation that seems to threaten our very existence.

But in the case of our systems developer, minutes before depart-ing for his manager's office, a remarkable, almost miraculous phone call intervenes from his wife. Barely able to get the words out of her mouth, she informs her husband that the lottery ticket they had purchased two days earlier held the winning numbers, and they have just won $345 million!

Now, many of us in these circumstances wouldn't even take the time to resign from our jobs in our haste to get to our car or train home. But in this case, as we put ourselves in the shoes of our developer colleague, let us consider how we would behave in our meeting with our bosses now that we have this new piece of infor-mation, now that we are one of the wealthiest people in the world.

Two minutes ago we were insecure, impoverished, and under siege. Now we enter the conversation more fearless and poised, coming from a place of abundance, with little to gain and little to lose. Before, we felt threatened and abandoned. Now, as a newly minted millionaire, we feel relaxed and confident, fascinated with our predicament rather than nervous about it. Before, we were prepared to make *our* case, highlighting successes and minimizing failures. Now we are curious about how our boss and the project managers will make *their* case. Less defensive now, we are prepared to engage in open dialogue—acknowledging mutual shortcomings, giving credit where it's due, and candidly probing difficulties.

As the meeting unfolds, we may still feel a bit scapegoated. But from our newly found place of abundance, such a victim mentality becomes an unnecessary distraction from engaging our circumstances. How comfortable is our boss in delivering the news? Is the conversation merely staged theater, or is a balanced picture being painted? Maybe, instead of defending ourselves, we offer reassurance. Maybe we smile as the "bad news" is presented and offer our former colleagues some unsolicited advice as we rise to depart the room.

And of course, saying farewell in such circumstances as a multimillionaire would be a matter of graciousness instead of desperation and embarrassment. We may even shake hands, express our appreciation, and wish everyone good luck rather than leave hardhearted and discouraged.

Now, the likelihood of a $345 million fantasy phone call somehow being part of our next inevitable troubling circumstance, whether at work or in our life overall, is unlikely indeed. But our ability to suddenly discover a powerful seat of fearless abundance may not be all that fantastic. In fact, rediscovering this fearless abundance is considered more likely than we think and is traditionally often referred to as "discovering the wish-fulfilling gem."

In Himalayan legend, the wish-fulfilling gem is a spiritual

stone hidden in the mystical kingdom of Shambhala that has the magical ability to manifest whatever the possessor wishes. The stone is often depicted as being held by celestial buddhas and bodhisattvas and is widely shown on prayer flags throughout the Himalayas as being carried on the back of a graceful wind-horse, or *lungta*. Discovering the gem is said to happen abruptly, like winning a lottery, thus opening up a sudden physical and spiritual energy similar to that of riding a mighty horse. This frees the mind of impoverishment and reveals the natural state of fearless abundance.

There are many profound spiritual practices for discovering the wish-fulfilling gem, and many traditions such as Qi Gong, Tai Chi, and Taoist medicine use the physical presence of the jewel to release the body's regenerative powers. In the tradition of mindfulness-awareness meditation, however, such a mystical jewel represents the natural expression of a mind that has been thoroughly trained in the practice of meditation.

Essentially, through years of meditation practice, we learn to *stabilize our attention* in the present moment, discover that we are *synchronized* and in harmony with our world, and then *see clearly* that our mind is a much vaster and more splendid proposition than we could ever have imagined. Gaining confidence in this discovery is like winning a $345 million spiritual lottery, where we are suddenly liberated from our hopes and fears and introduced to an utterly free and endowed physical presence: the natural state of fearless abundance.

For meditators, coming to this conclusion viscerally and completely is one of the great accomplishments of the practice. Sitting still hour after hour, day after day, year in and year out, we slowly and gently exhaust our futile struggle to secure our lives with paychecks and toys, emotional security pacts and addictions. And we awaken to a simple yet extraordinary fact of life: *when we stop struggling, we are free, confident, and at ease.*

Ironically, this abundance of suddenly discovering a wish-fulfilling gem within our very state of mind is a not a "personal" experience, so to speak, but something larger and more fundamental. Just as a sparrow flies with ease or a tiger walks with confidence, so too we discover the jewel-like ease and wealth of our humanness. A sparrow never second-guesses its wings; a tiger never arrogantly proclaims its stripes. And as humans, we relax back into our unshakable confidence that we, too, are exquisitely equipped to be on this planet *under all circumstances*—even if we don't win a $345 million lottery!

5

Command gracefully

ONE OF THE TRUE MARVELS of modern society is the impression of control we give ourselves moment by moment throughout the day. Touch a button and light appears, speed-dial a phone and someone says "hello," fly to a distant city while having lunch, flush a toilet, start a car. The list is endless and quite impressive.

Gaining control over our circumstances is a smart thing to do, no doubt. Such power is a brilliant and amazing expression of being human. But equally, such control can mislead us into misunderstanding our situation, where we *believe* we have control, but we don't; we *assume* we are making progress, but we are not; we *think* we are experiencing life, and we are actually out of touch. When we control our circumstances without appreciating the larger setting, we run the risk of cultivating disasters of all kinds.

If we pause for just a moment and take a true measure of our circumstances, we will notice that we have very little control over what is occurring around us.

The sky, which is apparently infinite in all directions and contains a vast amount of stuff, is obviously beyond our control. We can look into the sky, jump through the sky, throw things into the sky, but for the most part the sky is beyond our control. Gravity—things fall down all the time, which is really quite amazing. Objects are moving all over the place—trucks, tsunamis, mosquitoes, microwaves—sometimes helpful, other times dangerous: not much control there either. Thoughts—people are pretty much everywhere and they are having thoughts—some profoundly remarkable thoughts, some disturbingly bizarre thoughts, some basic run-of-the-mill thoughts. We have very little control over people's thoughts as well.

When we pause and consider our circumstances, we notice that our limited control, while marvelous, precise, and at times elegant, is delicately poised as a minor gesture in the larger landscape of our experience.

Taking this larger view is the natural outcome of practicing mindfulness-awareness meditation, where we no longer mistake our limited control for a vaster reality. Instead, we discover we are perfectly synchronized with this greater uncontrolled landscape, and as we instinctively blend with the melody of these boundless circumstances, we recognize that we are no longer *standing apart* seeking *control* but are an *expression of* the landscape and now have *command*.

Military strategists have been developing command-and-control theory for thousands of years, and there is much to be learned from their work on how intention, agility, trust, shared awareness, and much more shape our ability to influence complex circumstances. When it comes to leading a fearless life, however, we can take a more elemental approach, one best described in a short anecdote about a sparrow and a hawk that taught me an essential lesson about graceful command.

One of my favorite pastimes is watching birds of prey, and living in southeast Pennsylvania, I am ever on the alert to observe hawks, eagles, owls, and falcons as they hunt, nest, and soar. One fine spring day, driving along a country road, I came to a wide, freshly plowed field, and to my surprise I immediately noticed a small sparrow flying in open sky being trailed by a sparrow hawk. The display was breathtaking as the hawk mirrored the sparrow's every juke and feint. I just couldn't miss this ballet, so, noticing a truck traveling toward me, I pulled my car to the side of the road to fully savor the entire drama. As I watched the hawk slowly close the gap on his prey, the sparrow began an ascent that took her high into the sky in an elegant arc, with the hawk mimicking her every move. Then, as the sparrow descended arclike toward the earth, with the hawk within three feet of striking, she flew in front of the oncoming truck and, with exacting precision, careened directly over the truck's cab, just missing the trailer roof and leaving the unwitting hawk to be struck and killed by the fast-moving tractor trailer. The sparrow's elegance was immaculate, the sudden death of the hawk was stunning, and my heart both broke and marveled at such an astounding maneuver. And to this day I recall this drama for the many lessons it has taught me about living a fearless life.

Essentially, what I had witnessed that day was called, in military parlance, *shih* (pronounced "sher"), which is a central term found in the classic Chinese military-strategy text attributed to Sun Tzu entitled *The Art of War*. Shih, in brief, is how power shifts, focuses, and compels, and having graceful command over this ever-shifting shape of power is how we achieve effortless victories, as witnessed in our sparrow's remarkable ballet. While there are many lessons to be learned from this sparrow's victory over the hawk, her fearlessness sheds light on how to command gracefully with little but focused control.

Confident Instincts

When we are seeking to control our world, we want to have confidence *in something*: that our car will start, the spreadsheet will calculate, our employees will follow instructions. In the case of shih, when we command our world gracefully, we have confidence *as something*. Our sparrow was completely and utterly "sparrow"; her instincts were pure. She didn't hesitate or question her wings. She didn't try to negotiate or plead with the hawk. Her confidence as a sparrow was visceral and unshakable and she never wavered. In the same manner, being instinctively confident *as who we are—as a human being*—is the basis for commanding our lives gracefully.

Synchronized View

Our sparrow expressed a synchronized presence and was in touch with the contours of her world. The narrow impulse of her pursuer, the power of the truck, the symmetry of her arc—all were of a whole. In the same sense, when we as human beings synchronize ourselves physically, emotionally, and spiritually, inseparable from the greater landscape, we awaken to our individual presence *as* the wisdom of that greater landscape, which is the fearless view of command. Needless to say, recognizing such vast wisdom in one-self and others is more demanding, and simpler, than one might think, but through the practice of mindfulness-awareness medita-tion we discover that being synchronized—mind, body, and the world inseparable in the present moment—is how we *see clearly*. Traditionally this is called the wisdom of *lhagtong*.

Agile Presence

Despite the sparrow's obvious skill, her maneuver was greater than her immaculate timing and exacting precision. Her instincts were greater than her maneuver: she was part of the shapeless play, committed yet agile. The sparrow was predisposed as a presence, in touch with the moment as it arose, exploiting emerging advan-tages, and if the circumstances had changed, she would have adapted. She was not searching her pocket for instructions, nor had she mapped out her maneuver ahead of time (though orni-thologists have told me that such maneuvers from birds are com-mon and practiced). Living a fearless life is not about devising clever plans or holding on to success. It's about commanding gracefully—being a dynamic, agile presence that skillfully blends with what arises.

With such graceful command come warnings, of course. Being reckless and cowardly with such dynamics can cause enormous harm. Engaging the wisdom of shih requires that we train our minds to open to the larger sacred landscape and express our nat-ural gentleness and authenticity. Otherwise, we may end up fool-ishly abusing our world by stealing answers to a final exam, sabotaging a competitor, or even planting a bomb in a church or an airport. Such arrogance and cowardice is profoundly out of touch with reality and only heightens and prolongs the fear.

The slogan "Command gracefully" introduces the possibility of being profoundly skillful in living a fearless life. By synchronizing with our larger landscape, we move beyond simply controlling our world to working with an all-pervasive intelligence that offers command over the play of circumstances. Expressing such skillfulness in our lives is a sacred trust that we inherit at birth, and in the end, engaging life's circumstances with such agile, boundless wisdom is every human being's calling.

PART TWO

EXPLORING THE IRONIES OF COWARDICE

"Security is mostly a superstition. It does not exist in nature, nor do the children of men as a whole experience it. Avoiding danger is no safer in the long run than outright exposure. Life is either a daring adventure, or nothing."
—Helen Keller, American educator and author (1880–1968)

The nine slogans in this section invite us to examine how "cowering" in the face of life's challenges, threats, and insults more often than not authors the very struggles we seek to avoid:

6. Stop the "bubble wrap"
7. Mind the gap
8. Break the false promise
9. Reconnect
10. Don't count on it

11. Ask, "Who's kidding whom?"
12. Let it break
13. Nothing sticks
14. Lean in

When we mix these slogans with our daily life, we discover that troubles and crises invite us to make a fundamental choice: to bravely open to the experience with a noble heart or to draw our tail between our legs and seek false assurances. And by choosing to open rather than hide, we find that we are far better equipped to deal with life than we had thought.

6

Stop the "bubble wrap"

FOR A FORMER MANHATTANITE, there is no greater joy than returning to the familiar meadows and paths of Central Park, and whenever I visit New York for business, I try to spend some time strolling its endless acres. On one such sunny spring afternoon, I found myself wandering in the southern corner of the park across the street from the Plaza Hotel. It was a perfect day, and many tourists and native New Yorkers were out delighting in the play of city and scenery: couples strolling, young boys skateboarding, and old folks gently observing from park benches.

As I meandered down a slightly sloping footpath, I came upon what appeared at first glance to be the perfect family enjoying an afternoon walk. The mom and dad, hand in hand, casually smiling and chatting—a fine-looking, well-appointed couple—walked with an air of slow ease. And their two children, boys about the ages of six and eight, paraded ahead, one on roller skates, the other on a bike. In many respects, the family was beautiful to behold. Yet the scene remains vivid for me, not because of its ideal image but because of the profound sadness I feel whenever I recall that family in Central Park.

While at first glance all seemed in order, a closer inspection revealed a disturbing situation indeed. The younger boy on roller skates was in distress as he struggled to skate up the slightly inclining path. His skates had been put on safety lock, which meant that the wheels were prevented from freely turning, and the young boy was walking awkwardly up the slight hill, clanging and struggling as he went. His safety helmet was pushed back on his head and the straps pressed noticeably into his neck; his arms, outfitted with hand and elbow pads, flailed as he tried to gain traction. The sweat was pouring from his face, and he bore a look of frustration rather than exhilaration as his legs—they, too, outfitted with knee pads—shuffled uneasily beneath him.

The older boy, too, who was on the bike was having his troubles. Outfitted like his brother in safety helmet and hand, elbow, and knee pads, the boy was struggling to pedal his bike up the slight incline since the training wheels permitted only so much momentum. Like his brother, he, too, seemed to be fighting with his experience rather than enjoying it—awkwardly straining to get up the hill rather than delighting in the challenge. And as the two boys wrestled with their devices, mom and dad gazed on smiling: everything and everyone was in order, perfectly "bubble wrapped" with safety pads, safety locks, and helmets. In the midst of the ideal family moment, I sensed that something fine and handsome was being smothered.

Of course, this story is not suggesting we should be careless with our children and family members' safety. This is not about risking our health and well-being. Rather, living a fearless life will require that we examine a profound irony that we may have in common with this family in Central Park: *too often in seeking to protect ourselves from life, we end up suffocating the very thing we hope to preserve.*

The actor, afraid of failure, rehearses her lines one too many times, becoming wooden, and ends up masking her natural grace and mastery of inflection; the attorney, anxious about possibly being taken advantage of, high-handedly reminds all parties that he's "hard-hitting" and ends up missing the opportunity for compromise; the politician, uneasy about possibly being misperceived, offers banal talking points rather than authentic leadership. And yes, parents, seeking to protect their family from any and all threats, end up preventing their children from exercising the very muscles required for protecting themselves.

While such missteps often appear well-intentioned, the reality is that we are, in fact, chasing a false promise—the false promise of "bubble wrap"—that maybe, if we envelop our lives in endless assurances, we can escape the vivid reality that we, as human beings, are fundamentally exposed and that such exposure demands resilience, not suffocating assurances.

The slogan "Stop the bubble wrap" readily applies to leading for innovation as well. In an experiment involving 688 health care employees, researchers tried to determine what factors encourage employees to take risks and experiment with learning a new technology. The findings indicated that employees were willing to try various software applications and experiment with new system features when their managers openly stated that making mistakes would be OK and, in turn, did not punish employees for errors. In essence, managers said, "Go ahead, ride your bike without pads and bubble wrap. And don't worry if you fall . . . you'll be OK." As reported in the study:

> Contrary to conventional wisdom, allowing employees room to fail didn't diminish their performance. Indeed, the employees who experimented the most ended up being the most proficient and satisfied with the new technology—and the quickest to integrate it into their everyday work. They reported that they were able to use their time with patients more efficiently, which resulted in improved care.[1]

The slogan "Stop the bubble wrap" reminds us that we have a choice when confronted with the endless uncertainties of life: we can pull in, strategize, and "bubble-wrap" our emotions, our careers, indeed our entire lives in the hope that we can avoid life's inevitable disappointments, or we can stop buying into such false promises and instead recognize that we are already fully open and surprisingly well equipped to live life, with or without the elbow pads.

7

Mind the gap

WHEN I VISIT LONDON, I always enjoy encountering my favorite global warning, "Mind the gap": a caution to tube passengers to watch their step when passing over the space between the station platform and the train. The phrase and graphic has always cheered me up because it not only stops the mind in the midst of a hectic

commute but also reminds me to reflect on how to fearlessly face reality.

The first noble truth of Buddhism points out that we experience life's suffering in three ways: straightforward suffering, alternating suffering, and the confusion of conditioned existence. Now, the first two types of distress are pretty clear-cut. Straightforward suffering is the fact that it hurts to be alive—at times terribly so. Alternating suffering is also quite familiar: one moment we have our toys, life savings, jobs, and loved ones; the next, they are gone—forever. And as we all know, these two types of suffering can be catalogued endlessly.

The third type of suffering—the confusion of conditioned existence—is a bit trickier to recognize, and this is where the "gap" comes in.

Being human appears to be pretty reliable. The sun shines, our eyes see, our ears hear. Green is green and water is wet. Our circumstances seem consistent and dependable. But as we all know, things don't always work out. Gaps occur in our seemingly reliable experience: cell phone busy signals, misplaced keys, job layoffs, and sudden breakups, which alert us to a shapeless yet annoyingly untenable quality to life. Larger, more shocking gaps, such as earthquakes swallowing cities or roiling plagues that kill thousands, are so profoundly disorienting that we are forced to turn our heads in stunned bewilderment. Despite life's seeming order, we discover that our existence is filled with gaps: moments of uncertainty that reveal life to be utterly unpredictable and fragile.

For the most part, we would rather ignore gaps because they are so disturbing. We are annoyed, frustrated, and at times terrified by gaps because they expose a painful human inadequacy: no matter how hard we work at making life worthwhile, it appears that we are missing something—*it appears that we don't know how to be alive.*

So, instead of "minding the gaps," all too often we run away, hide, or simply ignore life's disturbing surprises. And in this modern society we work hard at it. Whether it's numbing ourselves with drugs or chasing false promises, blaming others or complaining about perceived injustices, or just entertaining ourselves endlessly with artificial distractions, we work hard at ignoring life's gaps, large and small.

Needless to say, ignoring reality isn't the brightest plan for living fearlessly. Instead, we can take the London tube's advice more seriously, and there is no better place to start minding the gap than at work, because it is here that we make the acquaintance of Mr. Murphy.

In one of my early jobs at the age of thirteen as a carpenter's assistant I remember overhearing my boss, John, talking to a truck driver who had arrived with a delivery of the wrong construction materials. We had been waiting all morning for the delivery, and when my boss discovered the errors, he was frustrated but resigned: "Well, it seems that Mr. Murphy's at it again," he said as he and the driver shared a brief smile. At the time, I wondered who this "Murphy" was and how he was involved in messing up the delivery. But things were quickly resolved and we were back to work.

Sure enough, a couple of days later, our truck got a flat, and while I was changing the tire, I overheard my boss remark to one of the carpenters, "Murphy's working overtime this week, isn't he?" And once again they shared a little laugh together. Before the week was out, Murphy's name was dropped once again when a floorboard cracked and needed to be replaced.

"Hey, John, who's this Mr. Murphy guy you keep mentioning?" I finally asked.

"Oh, you haven't met Murphy," howled John as he rolled his eyes wide and invited the attention of the other carpenters. "Oh, you need to meet Mr. Murphy. . . . He's our best friend. In fact, he's the guy who pays your salary. And Murphy's the hardest worker of us all . . . up early every morning and pays attention to every detail," John remarked with a grin as the others started to laugh.

Now, I knew that the guy who cut the checks wasn't named Murphy, and I was used to arriving early every morning and had yet to meet any Murphy on-site, so I was quickly getting a bit confused. And my colleagues could see it, which seemed to amuse them a lot.

"If you want to be successful in construction or any kind of work, Michael," John began to explain, "you'll have to get to know Murphy really well because you can always, always, depend on him. It's what we call Murphy's Law: 'Anything that can possibly go wrong does.'"

As it began to dawn on me that Mr. Murphy was more than just another guy on the job, John concluded, "And if you don't make friends with Murphy, well . . . let's put it this way, you'll end up being one frustrated SOB."

From that day forward, in all my jobs—whether as a truck driver, librarian, kitchen worker, teacher, or corporate executive—I noticed that there was no place better to learn how to fearlessly "mind the gaps" in life than being spiritually mentored by Mr. Murphy, because his sole job is to wake us up to the gaps of conditioned existence. In that sense, work is all about gaps and how we choose to engage them. Some of us panic when Murphy's computer system "gaps"; others patiently troubleshoot the problem. Some of us fret and worry when Murphy closes up business and we find ourselves laid off, "gapped" out of a job; others are resilient, adapting and finding options. Some of us throw tantrums, others parade in arrogance, and some of us crumble in defeat when Murphy shows up. Some of us even try having Murphy arrested, but no complaining or anger seems to be enough, because the gap of conditioned existence always remains vividly uncertain, challenging us to live life confidently.

The slogan "Mind the gap" reminds us that in order to live a fearless life, we must recognize life's uncertainties not as threats or inconveniences but as teachers who are inviting us to express our confidence, guiding us in how to live life properly, and while on the job I have learned that such a teacher goes by the name "Mr. Murphy."

8

Break the false promise

Turn on your TV, walk into any store, open any magazine, or gaze upon just about any purchased item and you will confront the art of the false promise. There are small, clumsy promises, such as the trite sexual invitations that accompany our purchases of orange juice and bath towels. Or there's the garish and utterly irresponsible promise of Las Vegas, where every sight, sound, and feeling is designed to cultivate false hopes. Or the ubiquitous "youth promise," in which we are told that smearing cocoa oil onto our toes and face will miraculously and tragically return us to our adolescence.

Our media-intensive society is brimming with lies—false promises large and small that suggest we ought to doubt who we are, that maybe we are incapable of living our life right here, right now, and that with a little more product, fame, entertainment, or glamour we could become someone else—someone more able; more attractive, happy, and fulfilled—a dangerous promise indeed and one that can and should be broken.

I first learned how to break the false promise as a freshman in college when I heard Paul Krassner, the famed satirist, and Ken Kesey, the Merry Prankster and author of *One Flew over the Cuckoo's Nest*, explain to a student-packed auditorium that, unbeknownst to everyone, the earth had been invaded by aliens set on taking over our minds. Using graphs, illustrations, and actual photographs, Krassner and Kesey satirically documented that we had indeed been invaded by aliens, who were cleverly concealing themselves among the population by resembling human beings. The aliens' intentions were to take over our television sets in order to sell us lies, useless products, and false images that would in turn transform us into aliens. Since most news announcers were aliens, Krassner wryly observed, we could in fact distinguish aliens from humans. Aliens, while resembling humans, looked oddly flawless; they spoke with a monotonous voice that seemed strangely staged. And they always had toothy smiles that were hypnotic.

As the hilarious yet poignantly discerning performance drew to a close, Kesey proposed a simple yet effective practice for defeating the aliens. He had tested it, he said, and it was fail-safe and required only two words and the easiest of gestures. But he was not prepared to share the technique with the crowd unless we took an oath to teach our children the practice as well. Of course, we all agreed, though most of us did not have children at the time.

After we took the oath, Kesey gave the following instruction:

"Sit with your children in front of the TV while a commercial of some sort is running, and together—and this has to be done as a family thing—together raise your right hands in a fist toward the TV screen, extend your middle finger upward, and shout at the TV the following two simple words: 'Fuck you!'"

It was a lot of fun rehearsing Kesey's anti-alien technique that night in the auditorium as he flashed pictures of aliens; many of us hadn't known at the time that President Nixon, Jerry Falwell, and Mayor Daley were aliens.

Krassner and Kesey's advice may be appropriate satire, and we may choose to follow their instructions on occasion. But just making fun of our culture of false promise is not sufficient, because it does not address the heartlessness, shame, and cowardice such lies cultivate.

Jean Kilbourne, author, filmmaker, and scholar, has pioneered research in the dreadful impact advertising's false promise has on the human heart, particularly in the portrayal of women:

> The sex object is a mannequin, a shell. Conventional beauty is her only attribute. She has no lines or wrinkles (which would indicate she had the bad taste and poor judgment to grow older), no scars or blemishes—indeed, she has no pores. She is thin, generally tall and long-legged, and, above all, she is young. All "beautiful" women in advertisements (including minority women), regardless of product or audience, conform to this norm. Women are constantly exhorted to emulate this ideal, to feel ashamed and guilty if they fail, and to feel that their desirability and lovability are contingent upon physical perfection.[1]

And such a sterile and artificial promise can have deadly effect. Anorexia nervosa, a psychological disorder affecting one out of every one hundred teenage American girls, drives sufferers to maintain excessively low body weight, often to the point of starvation. Employing extreme diet habits such as binge eating, vomiting, and misuse of laxatives, 6 percent die of the disease.[2]

Desperate to conform to an ideal and impossible standard, many women go to great lengths to manipulate and change their faces and bodies. A woman is conditioned to view her face as a mask and her body as an object, as things separate from and more important than her real self, constantly in need of alteration, improvement, and disguise. She is made to feel dissatisfied with and ashamed of herself.[3]

Of course, the slogan "Break the false promise" is not just about how false promises promote shame and doubt among young women. Gambling, drugs, pornography, cheap food—there are endless disgraceful seductions and never-ending stories of shattered lives. And in a sense, recognizing this widespread cowardly enterprise is the easy part. Appreciating the spiritual message underlying the suffering is the challenge: we chase false promises because we doubt who we are and feel unworthy to live our lives.

The slogan "Break the false promise" encourages us to be highly suspicious of the daily messages we receive offering security, entertainment, and success. Whether they are from Las Vegas or Wall Street, a soup can or a magazine cover, "Break the false promise" encourages us to remain alert, because beyond the blandness of it all, the culture of false promise is profoundly dangerous in its reck-lessness. For when we look closely at the promise, it is inviting us to feel ashamed of who we are—to overlook our natural elegance and power. It is a promise that we should be willing and able to break.

9

Reconnect

My first job on Wall Street was in the early eighties with a merchant bank right in the heart of New York's financial district. As a junior officer in a management-training center, I was responsible for making sure that seminars ran smoothly. My colleagues were smart and supportive, the training programs were top-notch, and I got to learn the ways of Wall Street from an unlikely perch: witnessing Wall Streeters learning from Wall Streeters on how to become better Wall Streeters. I learned many important lessons at my first "real" job in New York, especially the lesson to "reconnect."

My days started early, setting up training rooms, arranging audiovisual equipment, and generally making sure programs ran well. On one such morning, I had several seminars to set up— some more complicated than others—and I worked the early hours arranging room after room. One of the programs was a small group tutorial for three senior bankers on strengthening their presentation skills, and all that was required was a TV monitor and video playback machine, which I easily rolled to the front of the room and then checked off my list.

The morning was unfolding nicely, with participants arriving and programs starting on time, when one of the instructors rushed into my office clearly panicked and distressed.

"The video machine and monitor you put in my room are broken . . . they won't function at all and I have tried everything to make them work," she breathlessly announced. "I have three senior bankers sitting there looking at their Rolexes, and I have tried everything for the last ten minutes. Please could you help out here!"

I could see that the instructor was mortified by her circumstances and was silently seething at me. I was "sabotaging" her program and she was not happy about it.

Walking at a quick pace, we arrived at the room, and upon entering, the instructor set the stage as I inspected the video and monitor.

"I apologize once again for the equipment failure. I've asked that they send us something that works," she hissed as she glanced over her shoulder at me. "It will be just a moment."

While the inconvenienced yet uninterested bankers read their *Wall Street Journals*, the instructor continued her staging as I inspected the equipment.

"Look, we have already tried checking the equipment, and it's clearly not functioning, so could you please just bring us a new set?" she broadcasted ever so subtly so as to be overheard.

And it was at that moment that our eyes together fell upon the culprit: the monitor and video machine were not plugged in.

I watched as the instructor's face went from "poised under fire" to "bewilderment" to "ashen wooziness" to "sharp panic" in a matter of seconds. She was about to have one of the most embarrassing moments of her career, and I felt an urgent need to let her have it without me.

"I think this will do it," I said as I plugged the set into the wall socket and the video lights and TV screen began to light up.

I glanced at the sullen faces of the bankers as I left the room, closing the door quietly behind me, and I thought, "Well, at least it was a pretty good demonstration of what not to do when giving a lecture."

Of course, there were important lessons for both the instructor and me to learn from such a simple yet glaring misstep. But I recall this story more because it illustrates a painful and frustrating irony many of us experience when we lose touch with our natural confidence, when we forget to "reconnect."

Just like my instructor colleague, many of us spend time trying to "fix" our lives by rearranging, blaming, at times even throttling the circumstances we face. Day in and day out we routinely face endless challenges, whether it's a conflict at home, a disagreement with a business partner, or a seemingly broken TV and video recorder. And yet we all too often unwittingly seek to unravel such puzzles by "trying everything to make it work" when our attention could be more wisely placed inward. Out of panic, embarrassment, or sheer bravado we can find ourselves hurriedly offering solutions to problems that don't even exist when in reality we've simply forgotten to "plug in" with ourselves. And we end up frustrated with life, not because there is any problem per se but because we have lost touch with something very basic: our ease and natural confidence.

Being out of touch with ourselves in this way causes a lot of *dis-ease*, *dis*-tress, and *dis*-orientation because when we focus on solving the problem "over there," rather than reconnecting with what is over here, we develop anxious, dull blind spots that strangely author the very circumstances we fear. Maybe, as it was with the instructor, our nervousness blinds us to the obvious and we end up authoring the very embarrassment we so wanted to avoid. Or maybe, in our hasty desire to collaborate with a well-positioned colleague, we unintentionally ignore others less in the limelight, fostering the ill feelings and grievances that our efforts at teamwork were meant to assuage. Or maybe in our effort to simply make somebody's day cheerful, we try too hard, repelling the exact friendship we had hoped to foster.

The slogan "Reconnect" reminds us of yet another bizarre irony of cowardice: when we are driven by anxiety and speed, we become disconnected from our basic resourcefulness, blinding ourselves to what needs our attention and in turn making us career toward the very thing we are hoping to avoid. And, of course, we have a choice: rather than "trying everything to make it work," we can instead reconnect with our natural confidence—alert, alive, and skillfully present.

10

Don't count on it

MY FATHER WAS A STEAMFITTER, as were my uncles, grandfather, brother, and many male cousins. Like all these men, my father worked hard earning a living. Heating schools, building oil refineries, and tearing down massive, obsolete boilers—these men worked carefully with their hands and minds to build a world that functioned well for others. My father was a tough man who, like many other Irish Americans of his generation, wrestled life into order and shaped it to his will.

Part of my father's journey involved relating to money as an obsession. He had watched his father lose his job during the Great Depression and as a teenager had become the breadwinner for his family. He had learned early on as a child to fear the possibilities of failure, to dread the prospects of poverty, and to worry endlessly about a worst-case scenario. So my father spent countless hours throughout his adult life managing his checkbook and investments as if his very life and that of his family depended on it.

Because of his obsession, my father was not a confident man.

He was smart, reliable, and devoted—tender in his own way. He had an unshakable sense of right and wrong, always looking out for the underdog. But, underneath it all, my father was afraid of his life.

"Life offers you happiness and pain, Michael," he once said to me, "and if you can make it to the end of your life having at least fifty-one percent happiness, then you have succeeded."

And so he struggled—admirably, powerfully, and, in the end, futilely, to live life with a "scorecard," hoping for the best and fearing the worst, trying to be as confident as he could in a world that offered no guarantees.

I, too, became frightened of my life, not just in my corporate career or in trying to secure myself financially. But because of my father, I was able to see early on that my fear was of something deeper than just losing a paycheck, a job, or a savings account. My fear had to do with losing confidence in myself. And as a consequence, my fear resulted in strategizing my way through life rather than living it, securing my life rather than opening to it, arguing with life's circumstances rather than embracing them. My fear, like my father's, was about losing touch with my basic resourcefulness.

And so, like my father, I tried to keep score, trying to secure life's pleasures and joys while warding off its disappointments and insults. But eventually I found keeping score was not as black and white as it seemed, because nothing added up. The math just didn't work. The joys of life—getting married, being promoted, or buying a home—often turned out to be disappointing, and the disappointments—being laid off, getting divorced, or losing a friend—often turned out to be the best things that ever happened to me. Aspects of life that I took for granted such as breathing, reading, or just getting wet grew to be delightful while sought-after slices of life such as pleasant food, possessions, and wealth became strangely problematic. I discovered that life's scorecard was unreliable, and often ironically twisted, and that trying to amass 51 percent happiness was pointless. I learned to not count on it.

It's not so easy, however, to not count on it. We all, at times, want to have a deal with our world. Whether at work, in relationships, or with family, we expect some return for our investing our lives, something to count on: a paycheck, some joy, love, or security. Maybe we are lonely and feel abandoned by life, so we make a deal with God that he will give us solace or salvation and in exchange we promise to behave ourselves. Or maybe we feel bored and not sufficiently entertained by life, so we make a deal with the local "toy factory" so that we can nuzzle endless pacifiers such as drugs, sex, or TV and in exchange we forfeit our dignity. Or maybe we are angry at being treated so poorly by life, so we make a deal with everyone everywhere that in exchange for our poverty mentality they are to treat us with respect and maybe a little awe. Making deals with our world and keeping score seems so reasonable and appropriate at times, but such a scorecard mentality offers nothing but frustration and, in the end, is a coward's game.

The slogan "Don't count on it" encourages us to fully appreciate the futility and hypocrisy of our scorecard mentality. And we use this slogan not because we want to beat ourselves with spiritual rubber hoses or shame ourselves for our cowardice. "Don't count on it" is not about repentance or shame. Rather, we choose to examine our false hope of keeping score because it is noble to be so honest with ourselves—noble because we are confident enough to face the facts straight on without false promises, numbing toys, or emotional deals. Such confidence stands utterly on its own: resourceful and free.

In the end, the slogan "Don't count on it" reminds us that our fear of life's uncertainties is really about our longing to be resourceful. We keep score out of anxiety, no doubt. But also keeping score, in a deep way, is about our desire to live our lives well. We struggle to make life work because we inherently know it is our nature to be keen and courageous. And in my heart, I know this was what my father was searching for in his life each time he worried about paying a bill, each time he balanced his checkbook, and each time he paid my college tuition.

11

Ask, "Who's kidding whom?"

I FIRST UNDERSTOOD how it felt to be betrayed when, at twelve years old, I received in the mail "two hair-raising monsters that really grow." My friend Frankie and I had read in a comic book that we could grow monsters right in our home. And nothing seemed more fantastic, tantalizing, and productive for us to do than to grow gruesome friends.

When we sent off our mail order, we read that we would receive not only "two living monsters" but also a whole bunch of official scientific stuff with which to manage them: an "Astronarium" with "Hydro Trays" and "Aqua Gauges." This was exciting stuff! When we received our package, we retreated to Frankie's room to secretly set up our lab—we wanted to keep our experiment to ourselves so we could later unleash our creatures on the world and surprise everybody! OOOHHHAAAA!!!

As we slowly opened the cardboard box, we worked gently to avoid harming our monsters, but I began to wonder why there was

no clanking of test tubes and no scientific instructions pasted on the box. A small voice inside was wondering, "Has there been a mistake?"

"What the heck is this?" Frankie whined with his face scrunched up as he raised two cardboard cartoon monsters from the box.

And as he placed them on his bedroom floor, I felt stunned and abandoned: my very first feelings of being betrayed. Because all we had received were two six-inch cardboard "monsters" with what looked like some old Rice Krispies stuck to their heads.

"These are the monsters?" I moaned as Frankie read from the two-page instruction manual.

"Congratulations on your purchase of these hair-raising monsters. You can help your monsters grow their hair by placing them on a dish or hydro tray and spraying them with water once a day. Your Aqua Gauge . . . "

My inner voice was panicking. "How could this be? It was all spelled out in a Superman comic book . . . in black and white!"

"Lemme see that." I grabbed the box out of desperation and began to read over the instructions.

"Hey, you know what these Rice Krispies are?" Frankie excitedly announced as he inspected one of our new bogus friends. "They're grass seed! All we have to do is put water on their heads and they'll grow a head of hair . . . I guess. . . . " His voice trailed off, once again stunned by the con.

As the fraud slowly became obvious over the next five minutes, a small seed of cynicism found its way into our hearts: we had been lied to, abandoned, and made to feel like fools. And from then on, Frankie and I would never fully trust someone else's words. Luckily, we preserved a small bit of our childlike purity— we did in fact water the grass seeds, just in case.

While Harold von Braunhut, the famed con artist who sent Frankie and me those lame monsters, may have felt that he was being a playful capitalist, he nonetheless was betraying something very basic about being human: by using deceptive speech, he had broken a sacred human bond. But we can prevent such a misstep in our lives by asking, "Who's kidding whom?"

Now, don't get me wrong. The thrill of buying those bogus monsters and being a punch line in Braunhut's gag were, in many ways, worth the price. We all love a good practical joke. But such a betrayal, small though it was, at that early age was for me a warning about what was to come. For, like so many of us, I was about to embark on a life in which cowardly speech would be dressed up as persuasion, lies offered as trust, and arrogance presented as strength. And only now, after forty-five years, can I look back and ask, "Who was kidding whom?"

The priests who spoon-fed lies to us as children were cowardly, no doubt. And such condescending weakness is a trap for so many even to this day. But in the end—clergy and children alike—we all have been left misled and abandoned, so who was kidding whom?

The politicians of the sixties and seventies who paraded pretense as patriotism were arrogant, no doubt. And even today politicians continue to serve up banal theatrics as a substitute for inspired statesmanship. But in the end, through the wounds of confronting Vietnam, racism, and so much more, we all—protester and politician alike—ended up being misled into a tragic war, so who was kidding whom?

The advertisers who sugarcoat what is toxic with false promises, selling poisonous food, deadly drugs, and breezy violence, are corrupt, no doubt. And today we are addicted to endless digital impulses in our search for the next answer to a question we don't even understand. But in the end, we consumers have all been victimized and left addicted to something or other, so who is kidding whom?

And of course, in our modern-day political discourse we willingly substitute logical advantage for truth and smother one another's voices with false impressions. Such cowardly speech, whether in our schools, our churches, or our politics, and whether on television, through daily discourse, or simply in a Superman comic book—is so ironically demeaning because we are only betraying ourselves. We are only kidding ourselves.

The slogan "Ask, 'Who's kidding whom?'" encourages us to first become very familiar with this irony of how we betray ourselves through the misuse of language. All too often we frame issues, ask questions, or pronounce an opinion not to clarify an issue or to help one another but out of a need to feel emotionally safe. Such a feeling of safety is not about avoiding tigers or bullets but about avoiding reality. We aggressively inflict our speech on others out of fear, afraid of feeling wronged, humbled, dismissed, or insignificant. Instead, we deceive ourselves into feeling right, proud, satisfied, or dominant by using language to buffer us from our world, to ward off threats, and to keep others in their place. Such fear of being emotionally diminished crudely hijacks the dignity of our human discourse, and we can find ourselves happily betraying others and living a coward's life.

When we are willing to forgo the cowardly games of emotional one-upsmanship, we discover that human communication is a profound bond in which we touch one another, and how we choose to touch is how we choose to be touched. If we choose to smack someone with our hand, our hand is smacked as well. If we choose to kiss someone with our lips, our lips are kissed as well. If we choose to turn our back on someone, our back is exposed. If we choose to use gentle words, our voice is at ease.

By recognizing that we human beings are woven together through our communications, we can then appreciate how human speech—both verbal and nonverbal—is much more than mere words, for at its most profound level it is how we choose to live our lives together. In a very real sense, we create our world with our language. Say "shut up" to your neighbor and your world becomes angry. Smile at someone and the sun shines. Stare in fear at someone and clouds arrive. Say "I love you" to your neighbor and your world becomes gentle. We shape our world with language, and when we choose to lead a fearless life, such a sacred bond with others is not taken lightly.

The slogan "Ask, 'Who's kidding whom?'" reminds us that we have tremendous responsibility in how we communicate with others. Avoiding cowardly speech by refraining from harsh words, patiently listening to others, being precise in our language, and much more will express and promote the very human dignity we seek. But if we find ourselves selling others a poor bill of goods, whether it is cardboard hair-raising monsters or political lies, we should always remember to ask, "Who's kidding whom?"

12

Let it break

MOST OF US ARE quite devoted to our work—willing to do whatever it takes to get the job done, meet the goal, or close the deal. Such loyalty is a much-sought-after commodity in the workplace and in many respects is quite admirable. Yet, when we offer our "stick-to-itiveness" and loyalty blindly to an enterprise, we may end up concealing what needs attention and doing more harm than good. And under those circumstances, rather than getting the job done, we may need to "let it break."

I once had a consulting assignment with a physician specializing in alternative medicine who was highly regarded for his medical advice and well-being seminars. The doctor was brilliant and uniquely articulate, to put it mildly, but was equally arrogant, self-absorbed, and emotionally clueless.

As part of his health-and-diet business, the doctor had launched a publishing imprint, and in order to get it off the ground he had asked me to "work with my publishing president and see if you can get things on track over there."

When I finally met the doctor's "publishing president," Shannon, I had mixed feelings. Shannon had solid editorial background and to her credit had been a nurse-practitioner–midwife in her younger years, which gave her practical insight into the health-publishing space. But she was no "publishing president." Many of the books she was working on were written by "the doctor's friends," and her list more resembled a vanity press than a thoughtful pipeline of winning books. Besides working with the authors—or, in her words, "pampering them"—editing manuscripts and overseeing book design, Shannon was responsible for PR, website maintenance, and marketing. And her staff consisted only of two junior assistants. Needless to say, my first meeting with Shannon was an exercise in assessing the severity of a burnout victim.

"I spend my entire day fighting fires," Shannon explained. "If it's not an author calling to complain about a cover design, it's my boss sending me his friend's manuscript that he wants reviewed ASAP. I'm expected to map out and execute all PR, and each book needs a website that I have to oversee. Running this publishing business is just impossible—it's too much for me," she concluded in exhaustion.

"Well, maybe that's the problem right there in a nutshell," I suggested. "You think you are running a publishing business, and your boss thinks that he has a publishing president managing an impressive imprint. But in reality, maybe it's all a sham."

"You could have fooled me," Shannon protested. "I'm working fifteen hours a day, traveling on the weekends, and have pretty much given up my personal life to make this imaginary publishing business work. It sure looks painfully real to me!"

"Exactly my point," I responded. "Your burning yourself out, overworking, and doing twenty different jobs may give the impression that you have a publishing business, but impressions aren't reality. A real publishing imprint is staffed correctly, and the president chooses the authors. A real publishing imprint has a budget for PR, and websites are handled by experts. I hate to say it, Shannon, but you've been spending your time letting your boss pretend that he has a publishing business, and as you can see, pretending is a lot of work."

"So what am I supposed to do?" she asked, clearly annoyed. "I've got a dozen deadlines, events that I have to plan, meetings to attend. What's your advice?"

"Let it break," I said.

"Let it break, let it break!! That's your advice?" Shannon howled. "That's what I have been afraid of happening and what I've been trying to avoid!"

"Stop being afraid and stop avoiding," I firmly encouraged. "Let it be what it is. Just let it break!"

Now, on the surface, such advice may appear cynical or possibly even treacherous. But to say "Let it break" is not to suggest that we shirk our responsibilities and watch our jobs spiral out of control. It's not like being an air traffic controller turning off our control panel so we can watch jet planes crash. Nor do we stop rushing to a fire because we are convinced that the fire truck needs to be replaced. In fact, knowing what, when, and how to let it break requires tremendous skill and compassion.

In order to let it break, we first must recognize that our willingness to do whatever it takes to finish the job and accomplish the objective is a valuable resource that needs to be applied skillfully, not recklessly. When our perseverance and vitality are taken for granted, overburdened, or abused, they become our worst enemy, blinding an organization, its leaders, and ourselves to lessons that need to be learned.

When such circumstances require that we let it break, we need not be reckless, however, throwing up our hands in frustration or threatening to quit. Our timing and insight are vital.

The airlines manager, pressured to meet unreasonable flight departure times, typically allows customers held up by long security lines to miss their flights in order to log excellent departure stats. At some point, the manager should not be so reliable and should instead purposefully let it break, delaying a departure deliberately for the sake of the customers. How airline management responds will speak volumes.

The finance manager is expected to close the books each month, but, with no accounting support, works unpaid weekends away from her family. At some point, she should not be so reliable and should simply let it break for the sake of her husband and children who just happen to be home sick with the flu that one weekend when the books need to be closed. How management responds will speak volumes.

And maybe the "publishing president," who is expected to function as a personal assistant rather than a respected media professional, shouldn't be so reliable; maybe she too should let it break.

Unfortunately, Shannon did not take my advice to let it break and she continued working seventy-hour weeks. However, she eventually left her role disgruntled, burned out, and physically ill. And while the physician had several books "successfully published," the enterprise was not sustainable and ended up losing money. When I reminded the doctor that the prestige of having a publishing imprint is much different from actually managing one, the advice, not surprisingly, fell on deaf ears. He, like Shannon, had not learned the needed lessons.

The slogan "Let it break" reminds us that recklessly managing workplace perseverance and loyalty can end up masking failure as success, weakness as strength, and dysfunction as harmony. And rather than reliably maintaining the charade, then growing disgruntled and becoming burned out, we can instead let it break and let the facts speak for themselves.

13

Nothing sticks

Too often we can mistake our opinions for facts. Listening to any run-of-the-mill TV talking head, Wall Street know-it-all, or self-absorbed politician, we can almost see their opinions harden and freeze into "facts" as the words leave their lips. We can at times become so passionate about our views that we mistake logical advantage for truth, belief for certainty, and thoughts for reality. Misunderstanding our world in such a way can create enormous confusion, where the simplest insight can be overlooked and the most promising opportunity missed. We can avoid such blindness, however, by practicing "Nothing sticks."

"Nothing sticks" begins with becoming an "expert," which is not typically good advice when traveling the mindfulness-awareness path. But in this case, if we want to rediscover our natural fearlessness, we will need to become experts in *upadana*, the futility of clinging to existence, a word the Buddha used to describe the fearful state of confused mind. Essentially, we experience upadana when we become bewildered by our fluid, uncertain circumstances and mistakenly try to secure ourselves by clinging to physical pleasures, reassuring thoughts, fixed ideologies, and emotional props of all kinds. Traditionally, we can untangle upadana confusion by practicing mindfulness-awareness meditation, thoroughly feeling the hopelessness of clinging, renouncing its pointlessness, and learning to let go rather than hold on.

According to the Buddha, we become an expert in upadana when we gain insight into the defining irony of our fearful clinging, an insight that when appreciated at its very core offers profound wisdom and great relief; *our struggle to cling to life is pointless and frustrating for only one reason: there is nothing to cling to.* In short, no matter how hard we work to hold on to our lives, nothing sticks.

Such a statement at first glance may seem a bit disheartening or strange. The reason we struggle is that we are grasping for something we long for but that does not exist? Well, that is disappointing indeed. Yet if we pause and look a bit closer, we may discover that this is tremendously good news.

Typically, when we engage our world from the perspective of upadana, we desperately want our opinions to "stick" to our world so that things appear certain. We expect our world to be like a dartboard or canvas so our opinions and feelings about things can stick. If, for example, we are fond of our workplace colleague, Greta, we paint a pleasant picture onto her, recalling her fine qualities and accenting her playful style. On the other hand, we may come to dislike our neighbor, Gerard, and we treat his unbecoming portrait as a dartboard, taking particular aim at his poor posture and clumsiness. In both cases, we replace Greta and Gerard with portraits and we "stick" them with our stories.

Now, the good news of "Nothing sticks" is that our upadana versions simply cannot define Greta and Gerard. They, like all of reality, are not solid or fixed, like dartboards or canvases, and their shapelessness is far more accommodating than our fearful need to paint false portraits. By recognizing that nothing sticks—that life offers absolutely nothing for our versions to cling to—we not only cut our habitual fear and bewilderment but, most important, discover the possibility of genuinely trusting our experience, and this is not a minor issue.

For some of us, trust may be like taking a leap of faith: "Hey, this bridge looks like it's in poor shape, but I'll walk across it anyway and trust that it won't collapse and kill me." Or maybe we see trust as weakness: "Gee, I can't depend on myself not to waste my money, so I'll entrust my paycheck to my friend." Or trust can even be seen as an expression of fear: "I am giving you my love and placing my trust in you not to hurt me!" In the case of "Nothing sticks," trust is not a matter of blind faith, weakness, or fear. Rather, we trust our experience precisely because nothing sticks. We commit to working with the fluid quality of relationships because we know full well that sticking any fixed version onto our experience clouds rather than clarifies, distorts rather than illuminates, conceals rather than reveals. "Nothing sticks" introduces us to the possibility of getting a clear, unmistakable view of life.

In the workplace, being an expert in upadana and practicing "Nothing sticks" can be tremendously helpful to ourselves and others. For example, as a human-resources executive, I have interviewed hundreds of job candidates and managed HR professionals responsible for interviewing thousands, and I have found, over the years, that what distinguishes truly great selection interviewing is the ability to trust the experience of the interview rather than "interviewing the résumé." Too often, out of a natural desire to select the right talent for the right job, we can find ourselves simply "interviewing the résumé" and overlooking the human moment. Rather than trusting the fluid quality of the actual interview, we cling to a script and stick to the process and often end up missing what we are looking for: our candidate.

I recall in 1986 interviewing a young man hoping to be hired as a computer programmer for the back office of a Wall Street brokerage house. A recent graduate with a degree in Romance Languages, a newbie to New York City, and with minimal experience in banking operations, the young fellow, on paper, was absolutely not an appropriate candidate for the job. But when I met him in person, it became quickly apparent that this shy, newly minted linguist would not only be able to easily master any programming language but, more important, he was a natural innovator, which was exactly what we needed in our operations at the time. The candidate was hired and was quite successful in his role, and today, as an experienced attorney, he has founded his own promising business in California specializing in programming cutting-edge algorithms for object-relational databases.

Now, this is not to say that we should hire every job candidate that we have a hunch about. Finding talented performers who have a proven track record in mastering the needed tasks is what recruiting is all about. "Nothing sticks" doesn't contradict sound business practice.

Rather, by practicing "Nothing sticks" we learn to step beyond our opinion and instead trust that we can work with what we see, experience, and feel without clinging to our version. Such trust is the height of respect, since we are willing to appreciate others on their own spacious and unique terms with little interest in reassuring ourselves. Over time, we learn to see what and who is worthy of our trust, gaining confidence in who is reliable, discerning what information is precise, and recognizing what promises are firm.

In the end, the slogan "Nothing sticks" encourages us to trust our experience of this ever-shifting, vast, and uncertain world. And since nothing sticks, there is nothing to cling to—a true relief in the midst of a hectic life.

14

Lean in

IF WE ARE FORTUNATE enough to be reading this book in a safe and comfortable place, we could pause for a moment and reflect on how we feel when we are afraid.

Maybe we feel guarded, uneasy, and revolted when we encounter spiders and venomous snakes. Or, more horrifically, we may feel petrified and desperate at the prospect of marauders invading our home. Maybe we are mildly apprehensive about our boss's need to control, or dreading melanoma. How we feel when we are afraid is rich and varied, powerful and haunting, and life seems to be filled with endless possibilities for such feelings.

If we are to overcome our cowardice, we will need to explore the textures and edges of how we feel when we are afraid, because *leaning into* such feelings is the key to leading a fearless life. Let's take a simple, mundane example.

It's the end of the day and, as is your routine, you arrive at your local tavern for a glass of beer, but this visit has a different twist. This time as you arrive and begin to take your seat at the bar, you notice that you are sitting across from an attractive woman, who happens to be your former wife. For a moment you feel confused, which yields to panic, for while she has yet to notice you, it is likely that when she does, her anger over your past betrayals will flood you with dismal, cruel memories. In an instant, you see that she is cheerfully sharing a glass of wine with a man you recognize as your younger brother, and at that very moment he reaches over and passionately kisses your former wife. Startled and feeling a bit weak, you sense that life is about to deliver a profoundly agonizing, complex, and decisive shock. And right there in that lively moment of fear, you have a visceral choice: to *lean in* or *lean away*.

Maybe you decide to lean away, turning your head and slipping out the door unnoticed. Or maybe you let yourself be noticed and you lean in, registering their shock, and then, leaning in further, you smile and buy them a drink. Or maybe you lean away in anger and watch from a distance, stewing in resentment and blame. Or maybe you just lean in when they notice and you simply cry. In the end, the dilemma in the tavern—as with all feelings of fear—offers a simple, stark choice: to lean in or to lean away.

Learning to lean into life's insults and challenges, whether they are mere barroom embarrassments or especially grim circumstances, is about having the courage to be naked—entirely exposed. Instinctively, we want to lean away from our emotions in those circumstances, numbing ourselves to feeling devastated, threatened, or humiliated. Maybe we could hide ourselves with feelings of justified anger. Or maybe we could confront life's insults with feeble apologies or sharp logics. But such tactics don't really lessen the emotion's penetrating immediacy, nor do they let us genuinely connect with the circumstances we confront. Leaning in naked and fully exposed takes tremendous bravery because we are willing to feel the depth of our suffering and come into direct contact with the circumstances that appear to be threatening us.

Since life offers up endless opportunities to lean in naked and exposed, we need not go looking for such possibilities. Whether it's meeting up with our ex in a bar or facing our own death, we will confront fear in our lives over and over again. But in order to learn to lean in, we can work with some simple, familiar, and potent occasions to get "naked," lean in, and cultivate our natural confidence throughout our daily life.

Don't Fidget

Whether you're waiting in line for a cup of coffee, sitting in a meeting that appears to be going nowhere, or just riding on a bus, notice when you feel restless. You may unwittingly begin to fidget: playing with a pencil, humming to yourself, maybe rehearsing a story line over and over in your head. Such fidgeting is essentially a coward's move. Rather than leaning into our experience, we lean away because we are not sufficiently entertained; our experience is too sharp and we pad our nakedness with a fidget. In this case, rather than fidgeting, we notice our restlessness, stop, get "naked," and lean into the sheer boredom of it all.[1]

Embrace Inconvenience

There always seems to be a nuisance, a seemingly useless distraction from our "valuable" life. We may work hard to eliminate such things, but somehow we end up annoyed by something. The neighbor who wants to chat as you are rushing to an appointment, the cat litter that always needs to be changed, the missing toilet paper roll—as we recoil from such simple annoyances, remember that's a coward's move and instead lean in, embracing the nakedness of the inconvenience.

Stop Simulating Busyness

We have so many gadgets: iPhones, iPads, newspapers, wristwatches, headsets, laptops, Kindles. Whenever we feel the urge, we can check e-mails, send text messages, leave a voice mail, tweet our friends, blog, update, sync, and so on. While such tools and activities have their place, they are also an easy retreat for the coward, where we pretend to be busy and step away from life. Instead of simulating busyness and speeding from one gadget to the next, we can instead stop and lean in. Instead of playing at life, we could actually nakedly live it.

Transform Impatience

Stuff never seems to work. The door handle won't turn; the traffic jam seems endless; the computer sluggishly reboots. And we become angry, because the world won't behave itself. Such anger is leaning away into a coward's crouch, where we feel entitled to blame the world. By noticing our impatience, we can instead linger and lean in, feeling fully the simple fact that stuff doesn't work.[2]

The slogan "Lean in" reminds us to fearlessly rise toward life's rawness and uncertainty rather than pull away. Such a gesture opens us to exactly what life presents: struggles and joys, insults and wonders, assaults and delights. And we can cultivate leaning in by transforming our simple daily fidgets and complaints into opportunities to embrace life's demands. For it is right here, in the mundane moments of life, where we can learn to emotionally grow up and lean in. Such simple fearlessness will serve us well when life invites us to embrace its more exquisite joys and shocking tragedies.

PART THREE

TAMING THE MIND

"The very act of dealing with fear is attaining fearlessness. We don't do two things—first overcoming fear and then starting on the project of developing fearlessness. All the fears are not going to just magically disappear. We will need to develop stability and insight. Stability in itself is not sufficient. Feeling a bit more calm and relaxed is not sufficient to overcome the deep sense of anxiety and anxiousness at the core of our being. To overcome it we need insight, which, according to Buddhism, involves profound reflection on our lives. That includes looking deeply at our fear. Looking deeply shows us its nature and teaches us how to work with it."

—The Venerable Traleg Kyabgon Rinpoche

The six slogans in this section will explore how mindfulness-awareness meditation helps us tame our restless "monkey, rabbit, and bird" mind, introducing us to our innate fearless presence:

15. Keep your feet on the ground
16. Stabilize attention

17. Synchronize with the present moment
18. See clearly
19. Don't short-change yourself
20. Be vividly present

By mixing these slogans with our daily life, we gain confidence to extend the wakeful presence we discover in our meditation practice into our daily life. By retreating into solitude for extended periods, maintaining a daily meditation practice, and engaging contemplations throughout the day, we become relaxed and familiar with our innate well-being, which we then fearlessly offer to others in order to ease distress and inspire confidence.

15

Keep your feet on the ground

A TRADITIONAL BUDDHIST image found throughout Asia depicts a partridge sitting atop a rabbit, which in turn is sitting atop a monkey, which in turn is seated upon an elephant standing on the earth beneath a banyan tree.

The picture, entitled "The Four Harmonious Ones," illustrates a tale told by the Buddha to his disciples about how to honor one's elders and build a cordial and cooperative society. The bird, having planted the tree by dropping a seed many years before, takes the exalted position above the others, which, being younger in years, take lesser positions and in so doing support one another in their efforts to gather fruit from the banyan tree. The image of "the four harmonious ones" has been used for centuries to teach children and adults how to work together and produce social harmony. However, this image also offers instruction in rediscovering fearlessness within our minds and illustrates how the path of mindfulness-awareness meditation can guide us to keep our feet on the ground.

When we pause and contemplate "The Four Harmonious Ones," we may notice that the image of three lively animals precariously standing on the back of a massive elephant seems more like a frantic balancing act than a portrait of harmony. And it is here, in the seeming disharmony of the image, that we can explore its teaching on meditation.

When we sit in meditation, especially in the beginning of our journey, we notice that our attention is quite unruly and ungrounded. Sometimes like a bird, our attention can suddenly fly off in any direction at the simplest provocation. Our bird mind can seem so wild. Fluttering here and there—suddenly pursuing this thought and then the next.

Other times our attention can be like a rabbit's—tremendously alert and paranoid. One moment, frozen in recollecting and anticipating; at other times, dashing off at a moment's notice out of anxiety, our rabbit mind is quick, fearful, and panicky.

And then there is our monkey mind: very clever and ever on guard for an opportunity to acquire some goodies. The monkey continually grasps for some promising thought or memory that he can collect and savor. Speedy, constantly moving, tremendously alert, our monkey mind is only interested in what is tasty—everything else is to be discarded or possibly attacked.

Now, for many of us, these three styles of loosely attending to our experience is what we typically assume to be "our mind," and we experience this mind as an inner conversation that we have with ourselves throughout the day. Sometimes our bird-voice is anxious and touchy; sometimes our rabbit-voice is cautious and suspicious; sometimes our monkey-voice is casual, self-assured, and curious. And throughout the day we live our lives essentially anxious and on guard, inside our head thinking about our lives rather than actually living them.

Nowadays science has studied our three "friends," and research has found that permitting our bird, rabbit, and monkey mind to substitute thinking for actual experience makes us very anxious indeed. A recently published research paper entitled "A Wandering Mind Is an Unhappy Mind," applied smartphone technology in order to randomly sample people's thoughts, feelings, and actions and found that when our mind wanders from our experience, we are likely to conjure up and dwell upon thoughts that are more distressing than our immediate experience, creating anxiety and worry where none is needed.[1] In the words of the researchers,

"People are thinking about what is not happening almost as often as they are thinking about what is and . . . doing so typically makes them unhappy."[2] And when it comes to the workplace, our bird, rabbit, and monkey mind seems to spend more time avoiding work than actually doing it: "Employees' minds stray much more than managers probably imagine—about 50% of the workday— and almost always veer toward personal concerns."[3] In short, permitting our attention to wander, out of touch with our actual experience, fosters much of the very distress we hope to avoid.

But as we can see from the picture, there is more to our mind than just our three skittish friends. They all sit atop an elephant— strong, steady, and powerfully grounded. And the elephant, in turn, is standing on the earth beneath a vast blue sky. And it is here—investigating the elephantlike confidence, the earthlike immovability, and the vast sky of mind—that we may rediscover our human fearlessness.

The slogan "Keep your feet on the ground" reminds us that practicing mindfulness-awareness meditation reveals our minds to be naturally grounded. While we may be chasing birdlike thoughts or worrying about rabbitlike concerns, with or without our participation, our world is unfolding in undeniably vivid and penetrating terms that we can recognize and rest in anytime we would like. Such groundedness can transform our birdlike anxiety, rabbitlike fear, and monkeylike selfishness into a balanced, healthy presence. But as important, such elephantlike confidence unfolding out of our meditation practice introduces us to the earth we are standing on and the space that surrounds us in all directions. Rediscovering such natural balance to life and our minds is a profound and humbling wisdom: no longer distracted, but engaged; no longer fearful, but fearless; no longer anxious and drifting, but keeping our feet on the ground, we can actually taste the fruit of life right here, right now.

16

Stabilize attention

AT WORK, WE USE resources to get the job done: money, time, information, and tools of all kinds. And nowadays, the workplace values innovation and ingenuity to thrive in a fast-paced global marketplace.

Some jobs, such as housecleaning or garbage removal, require simple resources. And others require access to a complex range of devices, skills, and assets such as jobs in international diplomacy or deep-ocean oil drilling. Others, such as soft-tissue cancer research, demand ingenuity, while others, such as prison administration, rule out innovation of all kinds.

While different jobs rely on different resources in differing doses, there is a common resource that all jobs rely on heavily. Whether we are selling commodities at a trading desk or shoveling snow, teaching children to sing or repairing a steel girder, we all depend on the vital resource of human attention.

For many of us, human attention is something we take for granted. We speed-dial our colleague or e-mail our business partner and expect to get their attention and a speedy response. We go to our Monday morning meeting and present our plan, and we expect the people in the room to pay attention and follow through. Pretty simple.

But upon further reflection, we may notice that human attention is a more challenging dynamic than meets the eye. If we ask any high school classroom teacher or advertising manager about the challenge of getting and sustaining someone's attention, we quickly find that what we take for granted is instead an expensive, vital, and at times fickle resource indeed.

I am often invited to introduce mindfulness-awareness meditation in business settings, and unlike in years past, there is now a growing interest in how such a practice can be applied at work. Many people have read about meditation and are aware of some of the often-touted benefits, and not surprisingly, many expect to feel relaxed, calm, and stress-free at the end of a session. And some people do!

But what seems to fascinate most people when first learning mindfulness-awareness meditation is their inability to place their attention on their breath. The simple instruction "As soon as you notice you are thinking, label it 'thinking' and bring your attention back to your breath" seems, for many, to be an enormous challenge and puzzle. Our attention, which we take for granted in our day-to-day activities, when engaged directly in meditation is revealed to be fickle, restless, and uncontrollable.

The fact that our attention behaves like a frantic monkey or skittish bird or scared rabbit should come as no great surprise; however, when we consider the relentless pace of the modern display vying for our time and interest: cell phones, Internet, e-mail, five-hundred-channel TVs, digital displays—the list is long and growing. Little wonder that such speed distracts and disorients our attention, wasting one of our most prized resources.

In his *Wall Street Journal* (August 21, 2009) "manifesto for slow communications," John Freeman aptly describes our attention dilemma:

> There is a paradox here, though. The Internet has provided us with an almost unlimited amount of information, but the speed at which it works—and we work through it—has deprived us of its benefits. . . . Making decisions in this communication brownout, though without complete information, we go to war hastily, go to meetings unprepared, and build relationships on the slippery gravel of false impressions. Attention is one of the most valuable modern resources. If we waste it on frivolous communication, we will have nothing left when we really need it.[1]

Practicing mindfulness-awareness meditation, then, is how we learn to reclaim our attention so that we can confidently bring it to bear on our work and life when we really need it.

Essentially, when we stabilize our attention with meditation, we are learning to come back to now: very simply, very directly, and often very monotonously. This ability to remember to "come back" to the present moment is the mindfulness aspect of the practice, and it requires discipline both on and off the cushion.

On the cushion, we mindfully come back to and place our attention on an "object of meditation," such as the breath, a visual object, or a sound. Over time, this discipline unfolds when we're off the cushion, because we increasingly notice when we are distracted by thoughts and spacing out. As our mindfulness on the cushion strengthens, our attention off the cushion becomes more and more alert and precise in the present moment.

Typically, stabilizing the attention so that it does not wander from the immediate moment takes years of disciplined training. It is important to note that mindfully stabilizing the attention is not the goal of meditation, so to speak, but a foundation for permitting our natural fearless mind to arise.

The slogan "Stabilize attention" questions the speed and distractibility prevalent throughout our work life and calls us to take action: to reclaim the precious resource of our attention that is being hijacked by the marvels of modern technology. As John Freeman so poignantly sums it up:

[The speed of technology] has put us under great physical and mental strain, altering our brain chemistry and daily needs. It has isolated us from the people with whom we live, siphoning us away from real-world places where we gather. It has encouraged flotillas of unnecessary jabbering, making it difficult to tell signal from noise. It has made it more difficult to read slowly and enjoy it, hastening the already declining rates of literacy. It has made it harder to listen and mean it, to be idle and not fidget. This is not a sustainable way of life.[2]

Stabilizing attention, then, becomes our fundamental gesture for building a sustainable way of life; no longer mesmerized by the blur of endless distractions, we can come to our senses and "attend" to our world rather than breeze past it.

17

Synchronize with the present moment

WHEN WE ARE mindfully aware at work, it's not as if we are simply alert to the present moment, as if we were intently sightseeing or inspecting our experience. Rather, mindfulness-awareness introduces us to the reality that we are fully immersed—utterly harmonized, 360 degrees, with the circumstances in which we find ourselves. We instinctively take a panoramic view and become emotionally and physically in tune with our experience.

Let's take a simple example. One of the classic missteps at work is firing off an e-mail in response to a perceived insult or criticism. We've arrived at work a bit late and are rushing to make a meeting in fifteen minutes when we notice an e-mail in our inbox from the IT department entitled, "Your project is over budget, late, and is being reconsidered." We know the author—we've gotten these broadsides before, and frankly, we are a bit fed up.

We open the e-mail, glance quickly over the familiar criticisms, such as "we have some concerns," "there has been no follow-up," "meetings have been missed," and we fire off our curt response in bold capital letters: "PLEASE STOP SENDING THESE E-MAILS. IN THE FUTURE, JUST CALL."

We're feeling pretty good as we leave for the meeting, then we pause. A little flutter in our stomach tells us that we may have missed something and that we'd better just check one last detail. Reopening the offending e-mail, we check once again, and to our surprise we are not even the intended recipient. The e-mail was addressed to a colleague, copied to several senior managers, and we were blind-copied as a courtesy.

Such missteps often cause lasting damage at work and at times end careers. But by training in mindfulness-awareness meditation, we can learn to avoid such missteps if we "synchronize with the present moment"—learning to be fully attuned with our actual experience rather than just our version of it.

Typically, we experience much in our lives as "mental events." We "like" cherry vanilla ice cream, but we "dislike" sour milk. We "agree" with Rush Limbaugh, but we "disagree" with Douglas Fairbanks. We "welcome" praise from colleagues but harbor grudges about e-mails that appear to be criticizing us.

While such views may offer some valid insight or practical advice, they are nonetheless conceptual interpretations of the actual events we are experiencing. When we practice mindfulness-awareness, we become quite familiar with mental events and how they color our experience. In fact, the mindfulness aspect of the training teaches us to simply notice thoughts as they present themselves. In the meditation, there is no need to encourage, discourage, expand, or dwell on mental events. By simply recognizing thoughts as thoughts, we learn to distinguish between mental events and our actual experience. But what is our actual experience?

Discovering what we actually experience, whether it's at work or in daily life, begins with curiously exploring our circumstances and then noticing how our experience speaks to us. For example, let's consider a snowy winter day. Some of us may consider snow a hassle—a mess that creates chores and difficulties. Or we may see snow as a chance to be free—from school, work, routines. Maybe we enjoy watching snow fall or sliding down icy hills. Discovering our actual experience requires that we curiously explore our "snowy winter day" beyond such mental labels into that which is unknown.

We walk outside—maybe this time without shoes and socks. The snow falls gently and a crisp wind curls across the tops of distant trees. We bring our attention to *now*, relax all our senses, and, with no resistance, open to the entire situation. Sights, sounds, textures, tastes, and smells are freely perceived in the bright, clear presence of this very moment. And quite naturally we *synchronize:* our senses, our presence, and our "wintry" world arise as a wide fabric of being that expresses itself unmistakably. As my teacher, Chögyam Trungpa, describes synchronizing:

Synchronizing mind and body is looking and seeing directly beyond language . . . when you feel that you can afford to relax and perceive the world directly, then your vision can expand. You can see on the spot with wakefulness. Your eyes begin to open, wider and wider, and you see that the world is colorful and fresh and so precise; every sharp angle is fantastic.[1]

"Synchronizing with the present moment" is the natural outcome of mindfully stabilizing our attention in meditation. When the restlessness of thinking about life exhausts itself, we develop an awareness that our presence is already in tune with our world, experiencing a larger wakefulness beyond concept, opinion, and interpretation.

When we synchronize with our workplace, just like synchronizing with a wintry snowfall (with our shoes *on* this time), we become unavoidably alert for the full picture; we intuitively know that the stage is as important as the actors; we recognize an organization to be a web of lively relationships, not a series of isolated transactions about me and my opinions. When we train our minds in mindfulness-awareness, we become more and more aware that no matter what we do or say—whether in an e-mail or in the boardroom, in the cafeteria or at a press briefing—there is always a greater context to consider.

The slogan "Synchronize with the present moment" reminds us that we can instinctively open to a wider, wiser, and more dynamic immediacy than just our opinions. Narrowly focusing on *our* agenda, *our* insult, *our* needs, *our* job simply makes no sense when we are fully synchronized with a world that offers so much more. Being so viscerally in touch with our experience in this way frees us from victimizing ourselves and others with our rigid opinions, and by practicing mindfulness-awareness meditation, we increasingly realize that synchronizing with the present moment is not about making a choice but about recognizing reality.

18

See clearly

AT WORK, WE ARE interested in "doing" stuff—performing, achieving, executing, and accomplishing. We are all very familiar with these common workplace refrains: "What do you do for a living?" "What do I do next?" "Do they have enough to do?" "Don't just sit there, do something!" Work is all about "doing"— meeting goals and getting stuff done.

But work is not about doing just anything; we are also interested in doing stuff correctly. We want to make the "right" decisions, we want to be "accurate" in our assessments, and we want to execute flawlessly. So, for the most part, work is about "doing" and "knowing" how to do things properly. "Knowing" and "doing"— pretty straightforward.

For mindfulness-awareness practitioners, however, knowing and doing our jobs well, while vital, are not our primary responsibilities at work. Mindfulness-awareness reveals that for us to accomplish goals, conduct ourselves ethically, and contribute to our world, we must first "see clearly."

In my capacity as a business coach, I am often asked to work with executives to help them refine and improve their leadership abilities. At the beginning of each assignment, the executive is often eager to set goals, improve performance, and experiment with new techniques. But inevitably I have to slow him or her down and suggest a different approach.

"You know your job well and are pretty good at 'doing' things," I typically remark to the executive. "You wouldn't be where you are in your career if you weren't good at getting stuff done. So we are not as concerned about what you *do* for a living—you are already good at that. Rather, we are really interested in what you *see* for a living."

And it is from here—from how well we *see* the workplace, that we can confidently engage our challenges. "What are the top three most important business demands that your colleagues face?" "What unspoken messages are you receiving from your team members?" "How do your vendors describe your enterprise to others in the marketplace?" "What are people afraid of in your organization? What inspires them?" These and dozens of other vital questions are not about "doing" anything at all. What's required is a form of wisdom beyond just knowing and doing—what is required is to see clearly—to discern, recognize, and understand.

For mindfulness-awareness practitioners, cultivating this wisdom of seeing clearly is at the very heart of the practice. The discipline trains us to step out from behind the curtain of our restless minds and touch reality directly, getting a full, authentic measure of our experience beyond self-deception and impulsiveness. From this perspective, doing our jobs "correctly"—indeed living *our lives* correctly—is the easy part. Many of us know how to balance our checkbook, fix a computer, or perform open-heart surgery. The hard part is being skillful when engaging the many provocative, striking, and complex circumstances that unfold at work and in life in general: discerning what is hidden, appreciating a gesture of affection, grasping the intention of a paradox, accepting an unexpected invitation, celebrating a mixed triumph, learning from an alarming emergency—the list is endless, and it all requires that we see clearly in order to "know" and "do" intelligently.

For mindfulness-awareness practitioners, meditation is not about becoming more "correct" or "right" in doing our jobs and living our lives. Nor are we interested in becoming meditation experts, and thus becoming entitled to inflict our spiritual viewpoints on our colleagues, friends, and neighbors. We practice meditation so we can see our minds clearly—and not surprisingly, the more we see our own mind, the more we can see the minds of others. Appreciating other people's minds can be quite profound and poignant, where we see directly their motivations, aspirations, foibles, hopes, and fears. Such insight can be a sobering responsibility, and it naturally makes us more skillful and lively in how we accommodate others. By seeing ourselves clearly, we learn to see others clearly as well.

In a *Harvard Business Review* article, "Extreme Negotiations,"[1] the authors point to a vital talent that defines successful high-risk negotiators: seeing clearly—appreciating the hearts and minds of others. Reading about how soldier leaders obtain a clear picture in the midst of urban battle in Afghanistan, we learn from the article that Sergeant Dubay, confronted with a terrorist attack, took the time to see clearly, gathering much-needed intelligence before acting:

Dubay needed information fast. He could have obeyed his instincts and started making harsh demands. But he recognized the women's fear—and his own—and decided to slow things down, test his assumption that the women were collaborating with the enemy, and change his approach to getting the intelligence he needed.

He took off his dark glasses, slung his weapon onto his back and knelt just outside the room. He reassured the women that their homes were now secured by both Afghan and American forces and said he just wanted to understand why they were all clustered in this one room. Over the next 15 or 20 minutes he talked softly, acknowledging their fright at being caught in the middle of a firefight. Finally, one woman came forward and spoke about the men who had herded them into the room and then taken up positions. Dubay thanked her. Another woman spoke up. The men were not Afghan, she said; they looked like foreign fighters. Three or four other women offered details.

Dubay's courage to first see clearly before "doing" or "knowing" in this high-risk negotiation was critical to being skillful in a life-and-death circumstance. Rather than rushing to do what was right or expedient, the sergeant "slowed things down," "took off his dark glasses," and "just wanted to understand"—a fearless gesture of seeing clearly.

While most of us may not be required to see clearly while in hand-to-hand combat with terrorists, the practice of mindfulness-awareness meditation can support our efforts to appreciate what resonates with others. We know that being "right" or "expert"—

whether at work, in daily life, or on the battlefield—is at best half the journey—a journey that cannot be traveled alone. And because we explore our minds on the cushion, we are naturally curious about seeing others clearly and willing to slow things down, take off our dark glasses, and just understand.

The slogan "See clearly" reminds us that simply accomplishing our goals at work is not good enough without also accomplishing them skillfully. Whether it's meeting a sales goal, building a business alliance, or securing a village from terrorist attack, the slogan "See clearly" reminds us to avoid rushing past our experience under the guise of "doing the job" and instead slow down and recognize how to intelligently succeed.

19

Don't shortchange yourself

AT TIMES WE shortchange ourselves—in life, at work, and in our spiritual development. For example, as a business coach, I often pose this challenge to my clients: "Describe your life if you found your perfect job."

I get varying responses to this question. There is the Optimistic Cynic: "Oh right, the perfect job, where I have more money and free time than I need and I get to travel to beautiful places around the world. Exactly where do I sign up?" Or the Postponing Self-Defeatist: "I've always wanted to design this iPad application for pacifying unruly teenagers—but I'm not sure if I should work with my friend George, and I can't afford to leave my job right now . . . and besides, the likelihood is that. . . ." Or my favorite, the Narrow Pessimist: "The perfect job . . . ahh . . . like a job that pays the bills and gives me my weekends free. Boy, would that make me happy."

Over the years, I have found that many of us simply talk ourselves out of opportunities, saying no to the very prospects we are looking for: "No, I'll never make enough money"; "No, I can't leave my job, the medical insurance, and the 401(k)"; "No, they'll never offer me the job." Often, the first hurdle I help my clients over is how to stop saying no to themselves.

One client, a tenured university professor who had been teaching for over fifteen years and was responsible for numerous research projects and grants, had grown weary of the academic life and longed for more freedom and flexibility. He had been contemplating resigning from his prestigious tenured role to pursue a more rewarding career and lifestyle, but he had been hesitating, not wanting to leave behind all the benefits of university life. Once we got past the saying-no-to-yourself phase, the professor mapped a gently inspiring vision of his perfect job:

"Well, I'd like to work half the time and still make about the same amount of money—without all the irritating distractions of academia. And travel . . . maybe to certain parts of the world—like Nepal and maybe Haiti—where I could offer some services and also have new experiences. I want to spend more time with my wife and our grown children . . . and I have this pet project that will need a website and some resources, but I am pretty excited about it, and several universities have already invited me to pilot some of the training . . . and I want to have time to write poetry."

After listening and taking notes for about a half hour, I looked up at the professor and said:

"I don't want to sound flip and I know that fulfilling any personal vision takes hard work and sacrifice, but from my point of view standing over here and knowing what I know about you, this is a no-brainer. Of course, it will take planning and a lot of work, but you could have this way of life if you really want it."

And sure enough, after doing the math on income, insurance, and retirement and mapping out the likelihood that he could meet his salary needs through consulting and grant management in just half the time, it became apparent that what was ideal was in fact quite real. And sure enough, the professor resigned from the university, launched his pet project, and found more than ample time to travel, write poetry, and enjoy his family.

Just as with our careers, many of us tend to shortchange ourselves in our spiritual development, talking ourselves out of opportunities, saying no to ourselves, and avoiding the very wisdom we are looking for.

For example, for many of us, answering—even considering—the following question may seem unimaginable: "What would your life be like if you perfected your mindfulness-awareness practice and became a fully enlightened human being?"

Throughout my thirty-five years of practicing mindfulness-awareness meditation, I have struggled with this question. "No, it would be arrogant to presume that I could become enlightened . . . not me." Or "I have bills to pay and little time for practice and retreats . . . maybe someday . . . someday in the future, but not now." Or "How could I become enlightened with such a lazy, bogus mind? . . . I am such a loser . . . no way." For me, part of my journey has been noticing how much I say no to myself about fulfilling my practice.

In the Vajrayana and Zen traditions of mindfulness-awareness, answering this question is not an option but absolutely vital, right from the very start. And we answer the question not with words or speculation but with a direct and unmistakable experience of being a fully enlightened human being.

Now, for some of us, this may sound fantastic or out of the question or maybe even arrogantly naive. But the reality is that being fully human is not something we can postpone. We may chose to ignore who we are, pretend that we are someone else, or maybe even neglect the obvious, but being who we are is unavoidable—it's a simple matter of waking up. As the great Mahamudra master Khenchen Thrangu Rinpoche points out:

> Therefore, the practice of vipashyana or lhak tong meditation is very important. With regard to this, Jamgön Kongtrul Lodrö Thayé said that, although we all seem to think that the realization of the mind's nature is very difficult and hard to understand, why should it be? It is not the case at all that it is something far away from us, for which we need to search avidly. If anything, it is too close to us, because it is right here, right in our midst. And second, it is not because it is too subtle or too profound or too difficult to understand, that we do not realize it. We do not see it because it is too easy and too simple and too obvious.[1]

Traditionally, recognizing our inherent wakefulness begins with a glimpse or flash, called *kensho* in Zen and "direct pointing out" in Vajrayana, where a student and a teacher have a meeting of the minds and enlightenment becomes a very real experience.

It is no longer a myth or matter of speculation; we discover quite directly the sacredness of our circumstances, and it is from here that the fearless journey of mindfulness-awareness truly begins.

Once we are willing to acknowledge our inherent wakefulness, then how we live our lives—whether at work, with our family, adventuring around the world, or just doing chores—is no longer a search for enlightenment but a matter of expressing it. Cultivating this vigilance requires tremendous bravery and gentleness and can help us transform daily challenges into sacred opportunities. In the words of my teacher, Chögyam Trungpa:

> We need to cultivate . . . a constant experience or quality of sacredness in everyday life. Problems, difficulties, and challenges may arise quite suddenly in everyday life. We may have a flash of doubt or pain or an attack of emotion. At that very moment, at that same time, we can also have a flash of the sacredness in whatever arises, a sudden awareness of unconditional sacredness. It is very important to actually practice this and maintain it. . . . The cultivation of sacred world on the spot is the practice that allows all phenomenal experience to become part of . . . the basic enlightened structure of your life.[2]

The slogan "Don't shortchange yourself" reminds us that we cannot postpone who we are, whether at work or in our spiritual development. Especially if we are passionate about living a fulfilled, noble career, we can stop saying no to ourselves and permit our curiosity to explore and appreciate possibilities. We have nothing to lose in considering our vision's invitation. But more important, the slogan encourages us not to shortchange ourselves spiritually by postponing the opportunity to fearlessly live a wakeful life. We can express the natural outcome of our mindfulness-awareness practice; we can be humble and awake—there is no need to shortchange ourselves.

20

Be vividly present

WHEN WE PRACTICE meditation on the cushion, we take a specific posture: we sit up straight, shoulders back, chest open, relaxed and physically alert. Such a posture has been used in meditation for thousands of years by millions of people and is not arbitrary, though nowadays some people make all kinds of adjustments.

Modifying such a posture is unnecessary, however, because sitting in this way is totally natural and expresses that we are grounded in reality—fully present, without defenses, and fearless. And not surprisingly, a few social scientists have even noticed that taking such a posture communicates confidence and power in business settings.

In a recent study from the Kellogg School of Management entitled "Powerful Postures versus Powerful Roles," researchers found that sitting in an open, expansive body posture had more impact on how individuals perceive and express confidence than being given exalted titles or weighty roles.

In a series of experiments, the researchers found that subjects

who took an upright, expansive pose versus a constricted pose were more likely to exhibit confidence in making difficult decisions, to engender respect from others, and to respect themselves. The research concluded that "body postures (are) one of the most proximate correlates of the manifestations of power."[1]

Of course, the meditation posture isn't about collecting another "power technique" so that we can troop around the office like a master sergeant, chest out, shoulders back, projecting our power. "Hey, look at me! I am standing up straight and I am fearlessly in charge of you!" In fact, the fearlessness we discover by sitting upright and open reveals that we can be confident and gentle yet formidable in relation to our world and that we become familiar with such wisdom by noticing that we are vividly present.

"Be vividly present" is quite literally *being* our posture—that who we are is quite literally *how we are*—what my teacher, Chögyam Trungpa, called "head and shoulders." Essentially, when we wake up to our daily life, we wake up to the astounding reality that we are a living, breathing body functioning in the midst of vast, amazingly detailed space. We discover that what's awake is our bodily presence, not our mental tracking of it. When we are vividly present, we recognize that a grand arrangement has been gracefully unfolding with or without our mental noticing and that our physical presence is inherently expansive, sensuous, and awake. By taking our posture as a human being—our head and shoulders—we find that we are both vividly present and fearlessly enlightened.

In a sense, such posture is not "our" posture, so to speak—"head and shoulders" is all-pervasive. Everything—animate and inanimate, rivers, trees, animals, the entire natural world—is perfectly poised. When we are vividly present, we notice that everything in our world radiates the same fresh, penetrating bearing of head and shoulders. As my teacher observed:

We should feel *so good*. This world is the best world. . . . If you drive into the mountains with a friend, you may see the mountain deer. They're so well groomed, although they don't live on a farm. They have tremendous head and shoulders, and their horns are so beautiful. The birds who land on your porch are also well groomed, because they are not conditioned by ordinary conditionality. They are themselves. They are so good.

Look at the sun. The sun is shining. Nobody polishes the sun. The sun just shines. Look at the moon, the sky, the world at its best.[2]

The slogan "Be vividly present" points directly to the reality that our physical presence has been fearlessly awake all along and that by taking our posture on the cushion—upright, open, and alert—we can reconnect with this wakefulness thoroughly and completely. Off the cushion, "Vividly present" becomes our practice where we begin to notice more and more that we are vividly present *as* head and shoulders—we have an original posture, we have an original nature—upright, wonderfully alive, and utterly awake. And whether social scientists notice or not, such fearless bearing could never have been otherwise.

PART FOUR

ESTABLISHING A FEARLESS PRESENCE

"Fear is a natural reaction to moving closer to the truth."
—Pema Chödrön

The nine slogans in this section explore the noble emotions that we fearlessly express when we are willing to unconditionally open to our lives:

21. Dare to awaken *ziji*
22. Be, see, do
23. Gently lay down the burden
24. Where's the edge?
25. Take a straight dose
26. Be a spiritual fool
27. Hold sadness and joy
28. Be alone
29. Gather the fearless view

When we mix these slogans with our daily life, we discover that the old rules no longer apply. Trying to reassure ourselves emotionally, warding off life's disappointments, holding on to what makes us feel secure—all of these become strikingly pointless. And instead, we discover that we can live generously with a tenderness that is rich, powerful, and free. We discover a fresh way of emotionally being in the world by establishing our fearless presence.

21

Dare to awaken ziji

SEVERAL YEARS AGO, my partner, Susanna, and I were walking to the end of our driveway to retrieve our mail when we came upon a sign posted on our mailbox that read:

> Help!
> My name is Yankee and I am lost.
> If you see me, please call my family.

Along with the telephone number blazoned across the posting was a classic portrait of an overweight housecat, nose in focus, eyes wide and ears back, looking clearly panicked and trapped. Yankee the cat was lost and his family wanted him back.

As cat lovers, Susanna and I dutifully expressed our concern for Yankee and decided to keep a look out for our lost neighbor. And sure enough, later that day we did indeed glimpse the cat waddling through our backyard toward a small wooded area that houses our storage shed. We followed Yankee and found him curled up nicely beneath the outbuilding in the far corner, well out of reach but clearly visible.

After a quick call to the owners, a car pulled up filled with a beautiful family. From our home's window we watched as the father walked toward our door, head down and looking somewhat defeated. After the customary greeting, the father, with a deep sigh, thanked us.

"You don't know how much trouble I've been in," he said, nodding his head back toward the car.

"We're moving to Cape May in two days and somehow Yankee slipped out when I left the door open during the move, and since then the family has been . . . well, 'merciless' is the best word I can find."

"Well, not to worry, Yankee is out back. Bring your family in," we said, and in trooped a young mother cradling a newborn, with an excited five-year-old girl in tow.

"You found Yankee! You found Yankee!" the little girl cheered as her mother calmed her down.

"Yes, they found Yankee, sweetheart, and we'll get him back and make sure that he is never, ever, let out of the house again." The mother spoke soothingly, with a glaring eye trained on her sighing husband.

"Why don't we all go out back so we can help Yankee come

home?" Susanna suggested, trying to clear the air. But what was about to unfold was by no means going to clear the air.

The ritual started normally enough. The family crouched down to look beneath the shed and get a glimpse of Yankee, who was resting, quite out of reach, in the far corner.

"There he is, Mommy! There's Yankee!" the little girl squealed with delight.

"And Daddy will get him for you, sweetie," Mom insisted with a restrained hiss.

But despite the family's best efforts, pleading and cajoling for over an hour, Yankee was not to be retrieved.

The father prodded with a stick, while the mother cooed and pleaded. "Come here, you little Yankee poo-poo," she begged. Favorite toys, tantalizing strings, and bowls of cat pellets were offered; and the little girl kept calling, "Here, little kitty." But to no avail. Yankee would not budge; he simply crouched in the corner: smug, out of reach, and defiant.

"What do we do now, Mommy?" the little girl cried. "Why won't Yankee come home?"

As a last resort, the father pulled from his pocket a small packet of cat treats called Yum-Yums, got down on his knees, placed a few cat treats on the ground, and began to plead, "Come here, little Yankee Poo-Poo; here are your tasty Yum-Yummies. . . . Please, little Yankee." And the whole family chimed in: "Come here, kitty, kitty, kitty . . . come here, little Yankee!"

Once again, Yankee wouldn't budge—not even a slight gesture of recognition crossed his inscrutable whiskered mug. Yankee was going nowhere.

After some heated discussion between Mom and Dad and much comforting for a tearful daughter, the family departed. They were never to return, and Yankee was on his own.

I always enjoy telling this story because each of us, to some degree, has become a little bit like Yankee. Especially if we live in a developed country, we've become rather pampered, plump, and a prisoner to our cozy world. And maybe, like Yankee, we have been lulled into the life of a house cat, squatting occasionally in a litter box, preferring Yum-Yums and house toys over the rawness and immediacy of real life—losing touch with our original instincts.

But what makes Yankee such an inspiration is that he dared to walk away. Maybe he *waddled* away at first, but he chose, nonetheless, to leave behind an artificial life and instead fearlessly reconnect with something profoundly basic about himself. Rather than settling for tantalizing toys, stale food pellets, and catnip, Yankee dared to prefer his "catness" and to boldly embrace life on its terms. And despite not knowing what life had in store outside the shed's protective covering, Yankee was instinctively prepared to rely on his natural resources and skill. That day, when the family walked away and I glanced over to my new friend, I realized that Yankee had reconnected with something wonderfully fundamental—a fearless confidence that I had been searching for—and if a little fat cat curled up beneath my garden shed could do it, so could I!

Apparently, there is no single word in the English language that can adequately describe this deep instinctual confidence. Can a cat describe its own "catness"? Can water describe its "wateriness"? How does it feel for blue to be so "blue"? Yet despite such limitations, when it comes to being fully human, the Tibetan Buddhist tradition refers to this fearless confidence as *ziji*—a radiant, primordial dignity that imbues the very fabric of human life.

Nowadays, we are surrounded by artificiality, and life's rawness is often disguised as convenience. Whether we dine on mass-media hyper-pabulum, indulge in intoxicants to medicate ourselves through life, or substitute Internet porn for genuine passion, the modern-day cat bowl is filled with stale "tasty" morsels that help us grow fat and cowardly. And while slipping out the back door and hiding under the shed may at times seem appealing, most of us have obligations to family, livelihood, and society that demand another approach. For us humans, daring to awaken *ziji* is not a one-shot deal but a path that requires that we wake up to our fearlessness again and again and again.

Daring to awaken *ziji* requires us to step beyond our habitual mind and vigorously *feel* our lives directly as 100 percent human beings, and this can be done anywhere, anytime. Dressing in the morning for work, we gaze out the bedroom window to witness the sun rise once again, and suddenly, for no reason at all, we feel the vastness of being human—*ziji*. Peeling the rind off a garden melon, our hands wet as we savor a fresh, familiar, old joy—*ziji*. Walking the city streets on a hot summer day, we soak in completely the ripe smells of garbage and the smiles of young people flirting—*ziji*. Like our cat friend Yankee, we are utterly in the world—alert, self-reliant, intensely in touch with our experience: the coldness of "cold," the briskness of "brisk," the sadness of "sad." Awakening *ziji* is touching and being touched thoroughly—fully synchronized and expressing what makes us noble as human beings.

It's been six years now since Yankee fearlessly stepped out into the world, and he still lives in the neighborhood. Trim and elegant, he can be seen leaping fences, slyly cutting the edge of a summer field, or breezily observing his domain camouflaged beneath an autumn shrub. But all is not romantic with Yankee. He has had his struggles, witnessed in the bite-size scar below his neck and the delicate wariness as he approaches on his occasional visits. And on some snowy winter evenings I think of him, braving the elements in his underbrush den down by the pond. While Yankee has shed his waddle for sleekness and his panicked wide-eyed stare for a watchful awareness, he has also become tough, shrewd, and formidable. At times, it is clear that he lives on the edge of life and death.

For those of us who are inclined to take Yankee's lead and dare to awaken *ziji*, we may recognize that we, too, live on this very same edge. We may not need to brave the elements like the other 100 million homeless people in the world. Nor do we need to search out a daily meal like our 852 million neighbors who live on the edge of starvation. We may have untold resources at our disposal: clean water, education, technology, loving friends and family; for many of us the list is shockingly long. But despite our exceptional circumstances—or maybe *because of* them—we may sense that it is time to get back to basics and, like Yankee, reconnect with our fearless instincts and dare to awaken *ziji*.

22

Be, see, do

A CENTRAL PRINCIPLE of my seminars on Mindful Leadership is learning to "achieve nothing." Introducing such a possibility to business colleagues can be a lot of fun, because it arouses such passion and, at times, disdain. The entire notion seems so upsetting, so insultingly counterintuitive—the fact that in order to be an inspiring leader, we need to *not* accomplish, *not* achieve, *not* succeed. Yet, while such a suggestion as "achieving nothing" may seem utterly inappropriate, the practice of mindfulness-awareness points out in no uncertain terms that to lead a dignified life and to lead others well, we must perfect the effort of nonachievement—we must first learn how to simply *be*.

This is not to say that we shouldn't do our jobs well, complete our tasks, or strive for excellence, of course. We all have responsibilities and aspirations. Learning to "achieve nothing" is not about ignoring our life and the many challenges it presents. Rather, learning to achieve nothing is about recognizing a noble fact of life: we have fully and completely arrived right here, right now, and there is nowhere else to go.

By engaging life with such raw, simple immediacy, we discover that being fearless is not about becoming someone else—about achieving something else—but about being completely who and what we are on the spot. We establish such a fearless presence primarily through the sitting practice of mindfulness-awareness, but off the cushion, we express such wisdom through "Be, see, do."

Normally, our experience is more about do, do, do. Especially at work, our focus is almost exclusively on pursuing goals, hitting targets, completing projects, meeting expectations—we all know the score. And while such ambition is worthy, it nonetheless can be blinded by its own speed and forward-looking intent. When our focus is on do, do, do, we tend to treat work's ordinary challenges as annoyances, obstacles, or even insults. Basic business issues such as safety or ethics can be treated as sidetracks from doing, doing, doing. We may make the required gestures, publishing a code of conduct and performing our OSHA audits, but when we do, do, do, such business basics become rituals that just slow us down. Vital creative juices that stimulate innovation unleashed by humor, playfulness, and randomness become "nice to haves" on our path of do, do, do. And of course, the inevitable humanness of work—the emotional highs and lows, the camaraderie, the disappointments and successes—become marginalized rather than savored for their wisdom.

When we establish a fearless presence at work and in life in general, we permit doing to take its place within a greater field of confidence, where we recognize first how to be and see clearly, and our actions, then, become an expression of our wisdom rather than of our anxiousness to achieve.

Be

In the sitting practice of mindfulness-awareness, we learn to simply *be:* sitting still and *being.* Over time, by practicing such a discipline, we let go of our efforts to secure our life and recognize that we unfold as a simple presence—our mind, body, and the world around us vividly harmonized as a timeless immediacy. Such insight becomes the basis for living a fearless life, and the meditation practice is how we become increasingly familiar with such profound presence.

Ironically, living such a presence off the cushion starts with understanding "absence": absence of our versions, absence of our opinions, absence even of the names we use to label our world as this and that. When we *be,* we make the primary fearless gesture, removing our personal lens on life and noticing that our world is vibrantly fresh in nowness, yet utterly absent of reassuring concept or fixed certainty.

By becoming at ease and familiar with such absence, we establish how to fearlessly *be:* our lives, our jobs, and our every gesture, while utterly intimate when experienced directly, are fleeting, ungraspable, and penetratingly poignant.

See

When we establish the fearless presence of *being,* our senses, our mind, and our body are synchronized in nowness, naturally open and poised as a self-contained *seeing*. Typically, when we think of seeing, we think of a visual experience happening in our head area, just a little above our nose and mouth. But in this case, we are talking about *seeing* fearlessly, which is a profound form of openness, of bodily knowing.

In seventeenth-century Japan, there lived a profoundly realized Zen master, Bankei, who founded the "Clear-Eyed School" of Zen Buddhism, and in his sermons he persistently urged his students to make the simplest of human gestures—to "clearly recognize the Unborn Buddha Mind." Here, in one of his teachings, he points to the matter of seeing fearlessly:

> The actual proof of this unborn which perfectly manages everything is that, as you are all turned this way listening to me talk, if out back there's the cawing of crows, the chirping of sparrows, or the rustling of the wind, even though you are not deliberately trying to hear each of these sounds, you recognize and distinguish each one. The voices of the crows and sparrows, the rustling of the wind—you hear them without making any mistake about them and that's what is called hearing with the Unborn.[1]

And further:

> Since the Buddha mind you have from your parents is unborn and marvelously illuminating, before even a single thought is produced, all things are recognized and distinguished without resorting to any cleverness. Without attaching to notions of "enlightened" and "deluded," just remain in

the state where all things are recognized and distinguished. Let things take care of themselves and whatever comes along will be smoothly managed—whether you like it or not![2]

By *being* and opening to our immediate experience without conditions, we learn how to *see* fearlessly, "hear with the Unborn," and clearly recognize our experience for exactly what it is.

Do

Because we fearlessly establish our presence in nowness and open to our experience completely, we can then properly *do*—that is, skillfully conduct ourselves in the world and accomplish what is needed. Too often our *doing,* particularly at work, is an anxious, linear affair, where we rush to the finish line in the hope of success. However, when we act confidently from a fearless presence, going in a straight line toward our goals is far too contrived and limiting. When we *see* the situation clearly, we recognize that our conduct unfolds in a rich and intelligent context that shapes our actions *as* we succeed.

In the book *The Power of Positive Deviance* the authors document how difficult social problems can be solved if we step beyond the confines of do, do, do and widen our view to appreciate the intelligent context of our actions.[3] Essentially, the authors found that the standard model for resolving difficult social challenges, such as malnutrition, was woefully inadequate. Defining the problem, identifying solution-options, applying process, and measuring results, while fine for the linear mentality in the lab, missed the mark in the field, where real life required more openness and skill. Instead of applying solutions to achieve a result, the authors looked for positive deviants (PDs)—"outliers who succeed . . . against the odds"—and sought to nourish and strengthen such deviant behavior societywide.

One such striking example was in Vietnam, where 65 percent of the children under the age of five were malnourished. The government had few resources to help, and the vast majority of Vietnamese citizens lived in poverty, with little access to even basic resources. Traditional programs of distributing food via NGOs such as Save the Children had not worked, since the programs did not address the broader issues of child care, hygiene, and healthy behaviors. The "do, do, do" model, with all its good intentions, was not working and in fact was speeding past the very solution it was looking for.

The authors discovered that despite the dire circumstances, there were some children of impoverished families who were well nourished—the "positive deviants." Rather than trying to "achieve" success, these social scientists sought to *recognize* the success that was already in play. And what they found among the thousands of villagers were a few unseen innovators—those who had wisely and quietly deviated and in turn discovered the nutrition Vietnamese children desperately needed. Apparently, the mothers of the well-nourished children, unlike the majority of other mothers, washed their children's hands before meals and after tainted encounters. They also fed their children the shrimp and crabs from the rice paddies, even though such a practice was widely frowned upon. Furthermore, the healthy children were being fed several small meals each day, even though normally Vietnamese families ate only in the morning and evening. By taking in the same amount of food as other children but in smaller portions over longer time, the PD children processed nourishment more efficiently. By extending this wisdom that was already functioning in the system to the rest of the society, children's health improved in many villages, leading to a 65 to 85 percent decline in child malnutrition in over twenty of Vietnam's provinces.

In the end, the authors point out that pursuing a result can often blind us to the solution already being lived out before our very eyes and that by *being* patient and *seeing* clearly we can learn to skillfully cultivate the wisdom of what the authors call "unintended consequences."

The slogan "Be, see, do" reminds us that the practice of mindfulness-awareness meditation is about more than just calming our mind, relieving our stress, or becoming emotionally self-aware. By training ourselves in such a simple, raw way we can rediscover a vast, profound wisdom of *being* that opens and reveals a world where we *see* clearly exactly what to do in order to be helpful.

23

Gently lay down the burden

WHEN WE ESTABLISH a fearless presence, we discover that we are instinctively resourceful—able to respond artfully when adversity arises. Because we have synchronized our body and mind in nowness through meditation, we find ourselves feeling life's pleasures and pains fully, both the happiness and the hardship. We no longer have a callus on our heart, and we are now willing to fully touch and fully be touched. Becoming familiar with such openness is how we live a skillful, fearless life.

Opening to adversity in its many traumatic forms is no easy proposition, of course. Small difficulties, such as spilling a glass of milk on our iPhone, can seem so intrusive until we face a brutal tragedy such as losing our entire family in a fire. And how we react when adversity shows up shapes its contours and impact. Sometimes we panic and ignore our heartbreak by numbing ourselves, and then our trauma cuts us off from life's healing touch. Or we live a victim's life, where we blame ourselves and others and hide in embarrassment and rage. But when we establish our fearless presence, even for just a brief moment, we know intuitively that we can nobly embrace life's tragedies by gently laying down the burden.

On one of my most inspiring consulting assignments, I had the honor to work with a team of eighteen people whose sole job was to help homeless families find housing. Working out of a small office in the Washington, D.C., area, the team members exposed themselves, day in and day out, to the raw traumas of destitute parents with young children desperately seeking shelter. Each member of the team offered a unique perspective: a former construction worker laid low by a stroke who pulled himself back from homelessness to now offer others a helping hand; a mentally challenged young single woman who had decided that "at least I can help"; a Vietnam vet, sober for eight years and still slightly paralyzed from his war wounds. These were powerful people with powerful stories, and my job was to listen.

During my many conversations throughout my month with this team, I met a young woman, Touvé, whose smile and joyful, gentle presence was nothing less than astounding. As a thirty-eight-year-old single mother of five small children, Touvé had persevered through the most traumatic of life circumstances: losing her abusive husband to drugs, moving her young children across the country with no money, getting diagnosed with a debilitating disease, and then settling in a homeless shelter. Despite these almost insurmountable calamities, which occurred over a span of three years, Touvé rebuilt her family's foundation, becoming a manager of the women's shelter, renting an apartment, and regaining traction. But what was so astounding about Touvé wasn't her story but her glowing resilience in the face of such adversity; she had "gently laid down the burden," and I wanted to know how.

"How did you do it?" I finally asked Touvé in one of our many chats. "Most people are terrified to be destitute, yet you lived it and you continue to see the trauma each day, but somehow you seem to have thrived. How have you done it?"

"It didn't feel like thriving at the time, I can tell you that." Touvé laughed. "But having five wonderful children to love and care for helped a lot." She paused. "And you know, you do what you have to do," she quietly declared. "But I also discovered that being afraid of hard times was such a burden. And the weight was crushing me. I felt like such a failure seeing my young children without a home, without food, without hope. I had no husband, my family had asked us to leave, and we ended up in a shelter, which didn't feel safe at all. The pressure was breaking me."

"And how did you go on?" I asked with true shock and awe.

"Well, things shifted," she offered tentatively. "I just couldn't hold on anymore. My dreams were gone, my children's lives were in shambles, our hopes of being a happy family had vanished a long time ago. I had to let go and move on, I guess. And that's what I did." Touvé smiled warmly.

"So what did you do?" I probed.

"We built a new life. We started helping others in the shelter, organizing stuff, working together to get the shelter kids to school," Touvé recalled. "And when I finally found housing, they asked me if I wanted to continue working at the shelter and eventually I became a manager and now I am pretty good at this stuff . . . helping families."

"But you are so happy and cheerful. Why aren't you confused or addicted or in jail, like so many others?" I probed further.

"I'm not afraid anymore, I guess." She smiled. "I just couldn't bear the burden, so I left it behind."

In a sense, I wish my memories of Touvé's story could yield more explicit advice—a step-by-step program for overcoming fear in traumatic circumstances. But alas, that would be naive, since Touvé's wisdom was in her smile, her boundless energy, and her kindness toward others. Touvé's best advice was her fearless presence—visceral, unshakable, and clear.

Yet her words "I just couldn't hold on anymore" offered me a profound lesson in bravely and gently laying down the burden, because herein lies the deep sadness of being utterly fearless.

What was it that Touvé had to let go of? What burden did she "gently lay down"?

Like Touvé, we all want to protect what is precious in life: our hopes, our dreams, our family love and shared joys. We all have a childlike optimism, fragilely poised in a world that is so unruly. And like Touvé, we want to shield and nourish such preciousness, especially in our loved ones. We want our sisters and brothers to sing and be excited about life; we want our sons and daughters— all sons and daughters—to walk on a beach, to recite a poem, to laugh and marvel.

But life so often shatters such gentle optimism: a child killed in a car accident, an unwanted divorce, a friend who never calls, a parent who drinks in the dark. Or in Touvé's case, a family desperately derailed by homelessness. And, like Touvé, our grief in witnessing such discarded intimacies can be so large and unyielding that we could crumble under the weight of the devastating burden—unless we can gently lay down our hopes and dreams when they shatter and say farewell.

The slogan "Gently lay down the burden" reminds us that we can fearlessly travel into the vast stretches of grief where life at times brutally traumatizes what is fragile, tender, and precious. We can do such a thing because we are by nature fearlessly resourceful, making us able to touch the grief but also to let it go, to cherish what is precious but also to say farewell, to bear an unbearable burden but also to gently lay it down.

24

Where's the edge?

As a young man, I had the good fortune to study with my teacher Chögyam Trungpa Rinpoche in a secluded, contemplative setting high in the Rocky Mountains of Colorado. On one such occasion, I joined a group of about forty students to set up an encampment, where we worked with Rinpoche over five days studying the principles of mind protection, nonaggression, and decorum. All of us had been studying with Rinpoche for some time and were quite aware of how he expected such circumstances to unfold, and we all worked hard to flawlessly execute the arrangements: tents in formation, mess hall immaculate, meditation field appointed, daily schedule precise. Every detail was harmonized, and we were all quite proud of our well-organized encampment.

At the end of two days of study and practice, all of us met in an open field to meditate with Rinpoche and close out the day. As was the custom, we all wore khaki uniforms, while makeshift wooden benches served as tables for our practice materials. We looked quite sharp and disciplined, feeling at ease in our ideal setting as we quietly awaited Rinpoche's arrival.

Soon, however, Rinpoche's personal aide arrived, walked to the front of the group, and took his seat on a meditation bench. After taking a few moments to slowly consider the circumstances, he began his remarks.

"Well, what we have done here is quite remarkable," he said. "Forty disciplined men and women creating a precise world in a splendid meadow in the middle of the Colorado Rockies. We have established our Vajrayana presence according to plan, and things seem to be unfolding nicely for all of us." He smiled, nodding in recognition as others seemed to concur.

I, for one, was in agreement. "Life couldn't get any better than this," I thought, yet I sensed a slight twinge of concern dawning.

"But," he paused, sipping his water, and then, with a forceful, sharp roar he snapped, "Where's the edge?!"

"Where's the edge?!" he roared again, even louder this time, confronting all of us. "Do you know what I am talking about? WHERE'S THE $*&#@?!"! EDGE?"

In one brief second our harmony had been split open, and I felt our collective sense of bewilderment. "Where's the edge?" I thought. "Where's the edge? Where can I find an 'edge'?"

"If you people think you can hide in your tidy, little meditative world, everything neatly in its place and everything peaceful and well planned, then you have missed the entire point of coming here to study with Rinpoche." He stared fiercely at all of us.

"This is not about being good little boys and girls making sure we lull ourselves to sleep in some kind of false harmony. Where's your passion? Who's willing to take a risk? Who's a fool here?

140

Where's your playfulness and humor, for God's sake!!!? There is no harmony *WITHOUT AN EDGE!!"* he screamed this time. "Where's our edge?" he then asked gently.

We went on to have quite a memorable afternoon discussing how living a Buddhist life was about expressing our liveliness and passion, not about waiting for a teacher to do it for us; being exposed and naked, not safe and subservient; being sharply alive and playful—naturally awake, not comfy, tidy, and numb. For me it was then that the slogan "Where's the edge?" emerged as a defining principle for living a fearless life and courageously leading in the workplace.

Probably one of the biggest mistakes leaders make at work is managing for harmony. When confronted with personnel conflicts, mistakes in judgment, differences of opinion, or straight-on failure, too often we try to manage the situation by bringing about agreement, order, and "peacefulness." At first glance that seems to be appropriate—even obvious. Who wouldn't want some calmness instead of frustration, and agreement instead of discord? But more often than not, what is really needed when managing conflict is courage, not harmony.

In his defining book, *Managerial Courage,* Harvey Hornstein concluded from his research that seeking harmony in organizations, while worthy at times, was often a primary killer of innovation, initiative, and creativity:

> In an effort to achieve harmony, groups often homogenize individual behavior and opinion into undifferentiated, pale, inoffensive substance. In this way, consensus replaces diversity as a characteristic of the group's life. . . . Through a

succession of concessions, prompted by the desire to avoid conflict and achieve harmony, each person yields a little so that the agreements which result are no one's and everyone's. What often emerges under the pressure to get along, be nice and work and play well together is an uncontroversial package of rules about how to act and what to think, distinguished only by their blandness. . . . Individual acts of managerial courage often require "breaking step with the troops." They challenge popular, established practices and familiar routines. Courageous initiatives frequently spark conflict, disrupting organizational harmony. Such conflict is one of the principal organizational benefits of managerial courage. When properly managed, conflict focuses choices, aids commitment, elevates thinking and sharpens issues. Productive conflict, by continually juxtaposing organizational options, can be an enormous aid to organizational growth and progress.[1]

In short, when we overlook, avoid, or even dismiss the intelligent edge of conflict, we can find ourselves allowing harmony to anesthetize our creative thinking, clear seeing, and skillful action.

Rushing toward harmony can have a dire impact on how we develop effective teams as well. Bruce Tuckman's classic four stages for group development—"forming, storming, norming, and performing"—outlines the phases groups move through in seeking coherence and impact.[2] When a team is first formed, the individuals in the group initially test boundaries and seek to orient themselves and form reliable relationships ("forming"). Inevitably, such testing creates friction, where individuals resist group demands and limits ("storming"). Unfortunately, it is all too common for groups to avoid the brisk candor typical of the storming phase. Uncomfortable with the social risks, challenging emotions, and forthrightness, teams tend to ignore the friction, avoiding the edge rather than respecting it, hurrying toward the familiar routines and cohesiveness of "norming." Feelings and perspectives that needed to be fully aired during storming are instead repressed, only to arise later during the "performing" phase as unspoken resentments, simmering frustrations, or at times active resistance to a smoothly performing team. In the long run, when teams avoid conflict, they spend more time managing frustrations than managing the job.

Avoiding conflict produces a harmony of sorts, however, where we feel successful, as long as we are not inconvenienced and everyone behaves themselves. Being predictably polite, valuing process over accountability, avoiding candor—like placing plastic flowers in a motel room or wearing a clip-on tie to a funeral—we buy into a phony sense of prettiness and relief. Such mediocrity at work fosters cowardice, where we settle for being comfortable and free of irritation rather than impactful, agile, and creative. Over time, such complacency lulls us to sleep, and we become increasingly willing to ignore what needs our attention, avoid what needs to be said, and discourage what needs encouraging.

When we are courageous enough to engage in conflict respectfully, however, we discover that having an edge is an asset, not a problem. Rather than accepting a false harmony where frustrations languish just below the surface, our edge reveals a fearless harmony—a spacious kind of joy arising out of hard work and candor—like executing a perfect putt, tasting a finely balanced wine, or reaching the top of a mountain. Well beyond the mediocrity of mere comfort, fearless harmony is about appreciating and living the human edge—the richness of harmony, the fleeting joy of harmony, the elegance of harmony, the lusciousness of harmony. Such appreciation *demands* an edge—that we engage life's paradoxes and conflicts fearlessly, not as cowards or good boys and girls; and that we attend to what needs our attention, speak skillfully when we need to be heard, and encourage what is healthy and inspiring.

The slogan "Where's the edge?" reminds us that living in harmony is not about being free from conflict but about being free to live life fully. Whether we are practicing meditation in the Colorado Rockies or running a company in Seattle, we need not settle for plastic flowers or dumb down our inquisitiveness. Instead, we can live in fearless harmony with life, where the edge wakes us up and conflict invites us to courageously lend a hand.

25

Take a straight dose

WHILE I NEVER ADMIRED the former Alaskan governor Sarah Palin's style of leadership, I do have tremendous respect for her willingness to hunt for her family's meal. And while many enjoy poking fun at her self-promoting hunting videos, the fact of the matter is that she has actually tracked, killed, butchered, cooked, and eaten deer, elk, and other game. Now, for those of us who have done such a thing—and for the record, I have cleaned a few animal carcasses in my day—butchering and cleaning a dead animal is a very remarkable and powerful experience. Taking the life of an animal and then carving away its flesh from its bone, twisting through the sinews, and pressing through the stench and blood demands that we engage one of life's most unpleasant yet fiercely raw realities. Such an entirely human act—something we as humans have done millions and millions of times—ironically expresses a crude yet authentic reverence for life.

But for me and so many of us, such a raw and direct experience is, well, just a bit too inconvenient. We prefer going to our local grocery store and selecting the meat, freshly wrapped in neat little containers. And we want choices: chicken, beef, pork, or lamb. And understandably we don't want to be involved or even hear about how the creatures were corralled and butchered.

And some nights, when we are really tired, cutting and chewing the meat is too challenging, so we buy meat that is predigested—ground up into little patties. But even that, at times, is too much for some of us. So we buy those little patties of predigested meat cooked, and we eat them without even having to get out of our car. We just drive up to a window and someone reaches out and hand-feeds us a predigested meat patty. Life can be so pathetically convenient when we prefer.

Now, I am not suggesting that we all start hunting for our meals. We have far too many weapons discharging in the United States already. Nor am I against grocery stores. In fact, our ability to provide safe, fresh food of all kinds to hundreds of millions of people around the world is a true marvel, and the thousands of people involved in feeding the world's population each day are owed a debt of immense gratitude. What I am suggesting is that despite our best intentions, our relationship with being a human body—whether it's how we eat, smell, look, or feel—is constantly being hijacked by the false hope of convenience, but that we can ward off this hijacking if we "take a straight dose."

Taking a straight dose starts with being sharply honest about our modern frenzy to ward off the realities of being human. It's reasonable to want to be cool in hot weather, but when we air-condition every square inch of our lives, our humanity is hijacked by cowardice. It's sensible to want to relieve physical pain, but when we concentrate medicinal herbs such as coca or tobacco

into a powder in order to numb ourselves from life, our humanity is hijacked by cowardice. It's prudent, even inspiring, to preserve our youthful vitality as we grow old, but when we Botox our wrinkles and bleach our skin to con ourselves, our humanity is hijacked by cowardice. And as with our grocery store, it's perfectly reasonable to purchase hamburger, but when we speed past our lives in a rush for fast food, we forget that a life has been sacrificed for us, and right there, our humanity is hijacked by cowardice.

Clearly discerning how we betray our humanity in our addiction to modern-day conveniences sets the stage for actually taking a straight dose, where we fearlessly experience life on its terms, not ours. Making such a gesture is not a one-shot deal; it takes perseverance, precision, and courage. And when we practice mindfulness-awareness meditation, we are training ourselves in taking a straight dose. We sit down on a cushion, back straight, eyes open, and we purposefully drop our version of life and, instead, open to *this experience*, right here, right now, without any conditions at all: a straight dose.

There are infinite opportunities to take a straight dose, of course—for example, minor irritations such as a mosquito landing on our leg. We might pause and view such a minor irritation very precisely. Or maybe we are walking through a crowded restaurant and we notice the smell of curry and then we take a straight dose—we pause and savor the subtle aroma very precisely.

For me, one of the most vivid opportunities to "take a straight dose" is engaging with bodily fluids. I, for one, really don't like bodily fluids, especially the way they smell. And cleaning up feces, urine, pus, and mucus—these are definitely items I prefer not to deal with. But ironically, it was through these repulsive, yet very human, liquids that I experienced one of my greatest moments of love.

I was fortunate to be able to care for both of my parents in their old age as they approached death, and a few months before my father passed, I came upon him slouched over his bed gurgling in a puddle of phlegm and vomit. He had been lying in his mess for some time, and a quantity of it had become encrusted on his lips and face. As I roused him from his sleep, he awakened slowly, deeply frightened. As I comforted my father in his bewilderment, he began to sob sadly—he missed my mother terribly and upon waking had forgotten she had passed away. And now in the midst of this phlegm-filled mess, he recalled that his wife and best friend was dead, and he began to cry deeply. As I held my father, wet and stinking, he turned to me and said, "I love you for being my son and caring for me and Mom," and he slowly leaned toward me, phlegm and vomit encrusted on his lips, and kissed me on my mouth. Taking a straight dose that day was an honor indeed.

Engaging our humanity at such a crude and rugged level can be so simple and so beautifully revealing, as the Zen teacher and nurse-practitioner Sallie Tisdale so aptly describes:

At the end of our lives, we will find ourselves in the hands of others. I go to work. I cause pain, I relieve pain. I clean up vomit and feces and blood. I dig in, and sometimes I get disgusted, from somewhere down near the brain stem and the gut. I keep a straight face. I see how afraid people are of being judged in just that way, how devastating it is for them to confront the way their bodies crumble. They are so afraid that I will turn away, that they are no longer worthy because they are crumbling. But we are all crumbling, all the time.

Now and then, I think about Dogen dying, soiling his bed, being nursed by Egi, one of his female students. I imagine nursing my own teacher someday. I think of the Buddha dying from food poisoning, puking in his death bed. I think of myself washing him, his undefended, old body: his skin as fragile as fine paper, tearing at a rough touch, so thin I can see the pulse of blood along the veins of his hand. I imagine his wasted, bony body, the tendons on his neck standing out plain and clear as he gently takes his last breaths.

I think of Dogen and Shakyamuni, and all the rest, after this last breath—after their bowels relaxed and ran, and their bladders emptied and their eyes clouded over. I think of the flies arriving, and laying their eggs, and what happened after that.[1]

The slogan "Take a straight dose" encourages us to bravely savor life's delights and tragedies, paradoxes and marvels, pains and pleasures. The precision of taking a straight dose fiercely demands that we taste our world fully without betraying our humanity with predigested meat or numbing conveniences. We ache desperately at the loneliness of a friend and we celebrate the beauty of an autumn sky. We fall in love deeply and we grow old fully, with no need to disguise the fleeting rawness of it all.

For in the end, there is no need to lead an artificial life when the one unfolding right before our very eyes is so vividly inviting us to fearlessly wake up, drink deep, and take a straight dose.

26

Be a spiritual fool

SEVERAL YEARS AGO, a Canadian university invited me to give a lecture on spirituality and business, and one of the sponsoring professors was a spiritual friend who had studied closely with my teacher, Chögyam Trungpa Rinpoche. I respected my friend a lot and I was flattered that he was keen on introducing me to the audience of students and faculty.

When the time came for me to give the talk, my friend stepped to the podium at the front of the lecture hall to make some introductory remarks.

"Welcome, everyone," he began. "It is a great pleasure to introduce our speaker for this afternoon, Michael Carroll. Michael and I go way back." My friend gestured politely toward me as we exchanged smiles. "We have both studied in the same Buddhist lineage under the same teacher for over thirty years, and during that time I have watched Michael's career progress through Wall Street, publishing, and now consulting. And I have also witnessed his journey along the spiritual path, which I can say has one very distinguishing feature." He paused as he looked once again in my direction.

"In fact, I can say that Michael, of all the Buddhist practitioners I have known, has embodied a central principle that our teacher, Chögyam Trungpa, placed tremendous emphasis on."

At this point, I began to squirm a bit.

"Michael, throughout his entire Buddhist career, has never been afraid to be a fool."

I winced at being introduced to a hundred strangers as the biggest fool the host had ever known.

"Trungpa coined the phrase 'not afraid to be a fool,'" my friend continued, "as a core instruction for how to live a fearless life. And while many of us at the time worked hard at avoiding being fools, Michael was quite good at it!"

As the audience laughed, my friend and I shared a smile.

"And the amazing thing is," I said, interrupting, "now I get to write books about being a fool! The fun never ends!"

We went on to have a great discussion that day, of course, and I continue to be thankful to my friend for his humorous introduction, because being a spiritual fool has, in fact, been my journey all along. How many times have I had to sort out my arrogance? How many hours have I sat meditating without even noticing? How many times could I have extended a helping hand but didn't? How many years have I spent missing the obvious? If making one mistake after another is a way to travel the spiritual path, then I am an expert indeed.

Yet my teacher's instructive "not afraid to be a fool" speaks to more than just being a clueless knucklehead or a lazy narcissist. To be a spiritual fool requires that we expose ourselves to the great cosmic embarrassment: we don't know who we are and we desperately want an answer.

Such spiritual nakedness feels pure and healthy because it carries no pretense or smug spectacle, yet we feel awkwardly brave in admitting that we don't have the answer but deeply want to know the truth. Like falling in love, we become a fool for genuine passion. Like a child wondering at life's display, we marvel at the shocking scale and intimate detail—filled with a fool's innocent curiosity. To be a spiritual fool is to lead with our chin in a world that offers endless insults and disappointments, naively hoping to make a final and utterly authentic connection with our lives.

Such spiritual foolishness, examined closely, reveals that, as human beings, we are indeed instinctively fearless because we dare to feel lost—completely. We dare to emotionally acknowledge that we simply don't know how to resolve our most basic longing. And to step into such primal emotional uncertainty requires that we make spiritual fools of ourselves—feeling the rudeness of our mistakes and the embarrassment of our seeming inadequacies. Yet despite the anguish—despite the loneliness and fear—we discover behind such clumsiness a confidence that never questioned itself, since its intentions were pure and its longing so human.

My teacher Chögyam Trunpga so beautifully summed it up:

We have to be willing to be a fool and not always try to be a wise guy. We could almost say that being willing to be a fool is one of the first wisdoms. The phenomenal world can be perceived and seen properly if we see it from the perspective of being a fool. There is very little distance between being a fool and being wise; they are extremely close. When we are really, truly foolish, when we actually acknowledge our foolishness, then we are way ahead. We are not even in the process of becoming wise—we are already wise.[1]

The slogan "Be a spiritual fool" encourages us to rely on our raw courage and pure intention to discover exactly who we are. And along the way we will make many mistakes, look foolish, and make a mess of it. But to hide from such embarrassment, to shut down from being so emotionally exposed, is to cut ourselves off from the very confidence that we are seeking. Being a spiritual fool is about stepping out as a fearlessly exposed human being, which is exactly what we have been looking to become all along.

27

Hold sadness and joy

WHEN I WAS five years old, my parents very generously moved our family out of the city and into the countryside, where I was permitted to freely roam thousands of acres of Pennsylvania fields and woods. And over the years such freedom became one of the greatest gifts ever given to me by my kind and loving parents.

When I first moved to our new home as a youngster, I was only familiar with row houses and macadam, so the nearby meadows and ponds were truly fascinating. I marveled at creek perch and painted turtles, muskrats and pheasants, blue jays and bumblebees. I fell in love with nature, but from a distance.

One day, walking in the woods, I came upon a wounded sparrow. Picking the bird up with my bare hands, I rushed home in excitement to my father in the hope that we could relieve the small bird's distress. To this day I will never forget what it was like to hold that animal in my hands. I felt physically thrilled and in touch with something very old and vastly alive. I had never touched an animal before. Sure, I'd petted a dog or a cat, but never something wild, free, and breathing. I had met a great joy—something simple about touching life.

My dad, being very skillful with his hands, whipped up a little bird coop with chicken wire and a door. We placed straw and water and some grain in the coop and laid the bird on her side in the hope that she would heal. That night I went to bed with the excitement of a five-year-old; I could barely sleep for thinking about my new friend and praying that she would grow strong once again.

In the morning, I woke early and went out back to greet the sparrow, and there she was in the coop looking chipper and alert. I was delighted and, reaching into the cage, I gently gathered the bird into my hands and brought her out into the morning sunshine. Suddenly, without warning, my newfound friend broke away and flew off. And it was right there in that moment that I first felt the full exposure of a fearless heart: both the delight of knowing my new friend was safe and the sadness of suddenly saying good-bye forever. I cried and laughed at the same time, and it felt completely natural, as if the flight of a sparrow and a naked human heart were perfectly matched.

Now, the idea of feeling sadness and delight together may seem absurd. In fact, it often appears that holding life's delights close while warding off the sad difficulties is our only option. We are touched so fully by life's sharp edges and long, lonely spaces—at times, we may even feel terrified by the finality of it all, how life passes.

But, ironically, we hold sadness and joy closer than we think: the nurse saying farewell to a young patient who survived cancer; the farmer exhausted after weeks of harvesting crops; the dancer performing her favorite ballet for the last time; the beginning of a marathon, the birth of a child.

When we choose to live a fearless life, we enter this poignant territory where we recognize our experience as profoundly rich and emotionally wide open. And rather than resisting, we intuitively relax into life's spectacle, understanding full well that we cannot possess our experiences but can only savor them fleetingly. Such an emotional stance requires a fearless heart—a willingness to nobly expose ourselves over and over again to life's fullness.

We are all familiar with the fullness of a fearless heart. Our poets sing of it; our composers celebrate it; and great saints like Mother Teresa perfected it, as illustrated in this story taken from her 1979 Nobel Peace Prize acceptance speech:

One evening we went out and we picked up four people from the street. And one of them was in a most terrible condition—and I told the Sisters: You take care of the other three, I take care of this one that looked worse. So I did for her all that my love can do. I put her in bed, and there was such a beautiful smile on her face. She took hold of my hand, as she said one word only: Thank you—and she died.

I could not help but examine my conscience before her, and I asked what would I say if I was in her place. And my answer was very simple. I would have tried to draw a little attention to myself, I would have said I am hungry, that I am dying, I am cold, I am in pain, or something, but she gave me much more—she gave me her grateful love. And she died with a smile on her face. As that man whom we picked up from the drain, half eaten with worms, and we brought him to the home. I have lived like an animal in the street, but I am going to die like an angel, loved and cared for. And it was so wonderful to see the greatness of that man who could speak like that, who could die like that without blaming anybody, without cursing anybody, without comparing anything.[1]

Such nobleness is the very core of the fearless heart, and we need not travel to the streets of Calcutta to experience such tender dignity. All we need to do is step beyond our fear and make contact with reality. In the words of my teacher, Chögyam Trungpa:

Fear does not allow fundamental tenderness to enter into us. When tenderness tinged by sadness touches our heart, we know that we are in contact with reality. We feel it. That contact is genuine, fresh, and quite raw.[2]

The slogan "Hold sadness and joy" reminds us that we are constantly being touched by life. And if we have the confidence to step beyond our fear and to allow ourselves to actually be touched, we will rediscover our noble tenderness. Whether we are weathering a snowstorm, gazing at our grandmother for the last time, or letting go of a sparrow, this slogan reminds us that living fearlessly is a matter of gentleness, where delight and sadness, joy and heartache, shock and relief arise perfectly balanced together, inseparable. And it is here as we hold sadness and joy that we discover that we can live life confidently—we can hold such richness and smile and cry at the same time.

28

Be alone

WHEN WE LIVE a confident life, we fearlessly relax with our circumstances. Rather than trying to "fix" our lives, keep score, or defend ourselves, we instead recognize that life unfolds perfectly as it is. No matter what is happening—good, bad, happy, or sad—fearless mind is relaxed and open, embracing life's paradoxes and rawness, and almost magically the entire situation is freed from any struggle. Fully realizing such power is humbling and demanding, and traditionally one of the central instructions for doing so is "Be alone."

Most of us don't want to be alone. We love our families and enjoy working with colleagues. Neighbors, friends, lovers, and classmates—to be human is very much about sharing our lives with others and appreciating the intimacy of such relationships. And to be lonely—feeling abandoned and starved for friendship—feels so bleak and useless. Being alone, however, is not about abandoning our families or feeling worthless. Rather, it is about facing a simple fact of life: before we love or before we cry, before we invite or say good-bye, before anything at all happens, we first are naturally alone.

Such aloneness, when touched thoroughly, can feel a bit romantic, like taking a quiet warm bath or a stroll in the woods. Yet such intimacy of solitude is also powerfully grounded and gently confident. When we relax in such circumstances, we open and engage fully, the very root of a fearless mind.

Being alone is just about the simplest thing a human being can do. But relaxing with our aloneness can be challenging, and traditionally it is recommended to practice mindfulness-awareness meditation in order to develop the six marks of being alone:

1. Less need for security
2. Basically content
3. Avoiding unnecessary activities
4. No searching for relationships
5. Freeing up discursiveness
6. Friendliness with being present

Less Need for Security

Living in fear is recognizing that life offers no guarantees but insisting otherwise. Despite the facts, we are adamant that we are special, somehow immune from life's uncertain demands. Such insistence can at times resemble a tantrum where we worry and strategize, blame and bluff, hoard and harass. At work we fret about losing face, losing our jobs, or just losing out. In relationships, we agonize over love that is fleeting or lives that are fragile. In the end, when we live a cowardly life, we want to be special— we want a personalized emotional security pact with life.

Being alone, however, reveals that trying to secure our lives is not only pointless but moldy and stale, as if we were crouching in a closet without having taken a shower for months. Having the confidence to step out and stand on our own two feet, we discover a freshness to life's uncertainties and an emotional warmth to our presence. We are not deserving of "special" treatment, standing apart and above from life, throwing a quiet tantrum in a dark, stale closet. Rather, we relax into the rawness of everyday life and discover that we have less need for security because everything is sharply apparent.

Basically Content

I once had a friend who was addicted to the Home Shopping Network. She would compulsively watch the TV show, mesmerized by each new enticement. At times she would become deeply anguished in her panicked excitement over a "bargain." And flaunting her credit card, she would phone in her purchase with a newfound composure, convinced she was getting a remarkable deal.

For me, watching the sales pitches was fascinating. Each new piece of costume jewelry was showcased as a rare, once-in-a-life-time must-have. Each new useless piece of home furnishing was touted as exceptional, uniquely crafted, an uncommon find. Not once did the salespeople acknowledge that the little plastic crafts and porcelain dolls were more worthless than exceptional, more a rip-off than a bargain.

Such addiction to collecting "things" as companions is not uncommon in our modern society, but when we are willing to be alone, we discover that we are basically content with our circumstances as they are—without any bargains or salespeople. Our coffee cup is fine; we don't need another cup with our name on it or with a handle that is made to resemble a cat's tail. Our shirt or blouse is fine; we don't need to occupy ourselves with a bunch of companion shirts. To be alone is to be basically content with our physical setting—appreciative of the simple brightness of it all.

But that is not to say that the Home Shopping Network doesn't have some lessons to offer. To this day, I still learn from watching the show's crude, evangelical theatrics—a study in the art of fear and self-deception.

Avoiding Unnecessary Activities

Being afraid of life does not have to be as dramatic as cowering in a corner in dread, screaming at the top of our lungs, though some of us may feel that way on occasion. Fear is not always so dramatic. Rather, being afraid of our lives is, in many cases, far more careless and familiar.

It unfolds as simple, unnecessary gestures, such as fidgeting, humming to ourselves, or overchecking text messages, in order to avoid our lives. Or taking a pill or two to make our mind behave itself because the mind we have . . . well, it just isn't good enough. Distracting ourselves from a life we are afraid to live comes in many forms, some simple, some potent, some pathetic, others complex.

When we are willing to be alone, however, we stop finding excuses for avoiding our lives. Preoccupying ourselves with distractions and faux-gravitas agendas of all kinds becomes useless because when we are genuinely alone, we recognize viscerally that circumstances unfold quite well on their own.

No Searching for Relationships

There was a time in my middle-age life when I was enormously lonely. Circumstances had conspired so that I could no longer be with the ones I loved, and I spent many an hour alone after work at a local bar in my Upper West Side neighborhood in Manhattan. It wasn't that I felt sorry for myself or that I didn't count myself fortunate. I was just lonesome, yet quietly suspicious of my own reasons for feeling so.

Day in and day out, week in and week out, year in and year out, I would follow the same lonely ritual, but deep down I was really searching for a relationship. There was always a "maybe" in the air: maybe I would laugh with a neighbor, maybe share a story with a bartender, maybe meet a lover, or maybe make a new friend.

Of course, as an Irishman I have always felt that meeting people in bars is an excellent way to be human. But when we are willing to truly be alone, the unspoken hunger of "maybe" becomes unnecessary. The search for a relationship that may relieve us of living our lives becomes pointless, because when we are thoroughly alone, no relief is needed and relationships require no search.

Freeing Up Discursiveness

One of the great challenges of practicing mindfulness-awareness meditation is clarifying the busyness of our minds. On the one

162

hand we are able to notice that thoughts are just thoughts, passing phantoms that come and go. Yet at other times, thoughts unfold as a compelling story—*our* story, "The Michael Show" or "The Clarissa Show"—finely woven into an emotion-filled version of life that appears as "unmistakably" who we are.

At first, we may struggle with sorting out what is actually going on. We may try to eliminate some thoughts, analyze others, or ignore some altogether. We may try to resolve difficult emotions and protect those feelings we cherish. But over time—after meditating for hundreds, maybe thousands of hours—we drop such a struggle and become familiar with how we are noticing this display; we discover the natural calmness of our mind. To be alone is to become very familiar with this calmness—a natural ease of being.

When we are genuinely alone in this way, our discursiveness is freed up and our thoughts no longer unfold as unyielding opinion or solid self-impression. Since we are no longer amplifying or dumbing down emotions, we lighten up and experience our emotions and thoughts as a natural expression of being alone.

Friendliness with Being Present

At some point, we all have to make friends with our situation, and that begins with noticing there is nowhere else to go. As Michael McDonald so fittingly sang in 1979, "This is it, make no mistake where you are . . . the waiting is over." We may wish that we were three inches taller or had an extra $4,500 in our pocket. Or maybe we would have preferred that our sister didn't die of cancer or that our marriage could have worked out. But in the end, when we are willing to be alone, we have to admit that "This is it . . . the waiting is over."

When we have the courage to acknowledge and embrace the simple fact that there is nowhere else to go and no one else to become, we discover how to be friendly toward ourselves and toward the present moment. Traditionally, such an attitude is called *pakyang*—which in Tibetan means "childlike carefreeness"—utterly let loose and liberated. To be alone, then, is to make no mistake where we are and in turn to rediscover our natural freedom—our *pakyang*—becoming perfectly familiar with living in the present moment.

The slogan "Be alone" reminds us that when we stop trying to distract ourselves from our lives, we find that we are naturally and vibrantly alone. While such a prospect may appear troubling, the reality is that such aloneness is fresh, awake, and open—the very ground for developing a fearless mind.

Traditionally, to develop the six marks of being alone, it is highly recommended that we retreat into solitude on occasion for extended periods of focused mindfulness-awareness meditation. In appendix F, I suggest several retreat centers that offer extended solitary retreats.

29

Gather the fearless view

As HUMAN BEINGS, we naturally take postures that offer us various views of life. If we are repairing a broken heart or teaching a child to sing, our position as a therapist or voice teacher offers us a unique view so we can skillfully heal or teach. And if we are a CEO or parent, our position of authority offers us a privileged view in order to care for our world. This interplay between position and view is central to conducting ourselves skillfully in the world, and when we confidently establish our presence, we learn how to "Gather the fearless view."

> The eagle settles on a singular cedar branch.
> The tiger rests in a fiercely shaded grove.
> And the human heart conjures a greater wonder
> By arranging the world elegantly.

The Eagle Settles on a Singular Cedar Branch

Eagles, like most birds of prey, are remarkably artful in observing their world. Whether circling from above, settling on a familiar tree branch, or resting on a cliff's edge, they observe from locations where they can gather the widest view of their circumstances. Built to observe their world strategically, eagles naturally establish their presence and command. Just so, when we establish our fearless presence, we learn to take the widest view of life.

A newborn is stunning to gaze upon, no doubt. But the wide view sees old age and death at the same time. Resolving a difficult conflict has its rewards, of course. But the wide view knows that another conflict is about to arise. Being promoted to president or tenured professor is refreshing, but the wide view senses the long road ahead. When we take an eagle's wide view, closing the deal includes losing the deal; falling in love includes a broken heart. Such a view sees the stage as well as the actors, the river's beginning as well as its end.

By taking such a wide, eaglelike view of life, we step beyond the narrow safety of a coward's perspective and dare to recognize the vast, magnificent contours of reality. And, like the eagle, with such a fearless view we engage life with powerful confidence.

The Tiger Rests in a Fiercely Shaded Grove

Though I have never had the good fortune to observe tigers in the wild, we know that, in general, tigers spend sixteen plus hours a day resting in shaded areas. There are practical reasons for such lolling about, of course, such as preserving energy for the hunt and staying out of the heat. But tigers can be said to rest in fiercely shaded groves because as they rest unchallenged, they take a fearless view that commands their world.

For example, wandering thoughtlessly through a tiger's grove would not be a bright thing to do, since such carelessness would instantly transform the tiger from peaceful rest to fierce presence, and us from bumbling tourist to afternoon snack. Just so, when we establish our fearless presence, we take a relaxed yet formidable view from a position of power that leaves little room for recklessness.

We may be sipping a cocktail while speaking with the president of South Africa about curing AIDS, but we know when to put the glass down and we never spill a drop. We may be a "mere" consultant on a project, but our expertise, intelligently and precisely offered, awakens intelligence and precision in return. We may be negotiating a difficult contract, but our opponent is well aware that cavalierly exploiting our weak points would be a misstep.

When we take the fierce, tigerlike view of life, we step beyond the careless anxiety of hope and fear and instead project a relaxed yet precise presence, and from such a fearless view, we engage life vigorously while at ease.

And the Human Heart Conjures a Greater Wonder

Soaring elegantly, the eagle's sky dance is awe-inspiring; blending into the bamboo shadows, the tiger's presence is breathtaking. When gathering the fearless view, we humans take such an open and formidable posture that in turn rouses a greater wonder beyond the view: we gather and shape our world.

Rembrandt's portraits and Franklin's electricity, woven wool and hammered iron, ballroom dancing and jazz music—as human beings, our view of life liberates and celebrates the wonder inherent within the display. By being curious about our world, we naturally arrange it to produce laundry and friendships, music and gardens, skyscrapers and food.

We can consider such rousing human energy as "wonder," not because we are looking for some entertainment but because the fearless view reveals, recognizes, and displays life's awesome sacredness. Here this greater-striking wonder that arises out of the fearless human heart is our ability to transform our world—to stir forces, evoke marvels, and shape raw, natural substance at our command.

By Arranging the World Elegantly

Whether we are building a home, plowing a field, creating a road, or disposing of garbage, gathering the fearless view reveals our physical world as sacred. Rather than being out of touch, we keenly observe how time, earth, and space blend, guiding us in conjuring our remarkable human existence.

At the curve of a river, men and women gather to trade, and over thousands of years Rome unfolds. A father gives his sons a toy that they cherish and transform into modern-day aviation. Two mates quit college, do some brilliant math in a garage, and end up placing the entire history of human knowledge into the hands of every man, woman, and child on earth. Or more simply, we purchase a radiant turquoise bracelet and offer it as a gift to our child on graduation day. Such gestures of conjuring our world, all simple and vast at the same time, are the wonder of an aroused human heart, and by gathering the fearless view, we orient ourselves toward this elegance, evoking the noble energies of our world.

The slogan "Gather the fearless view" reminds us that we are born perfectly positioned to recognize the vast, magnificent wonder of reality. And from such a view we can build a global business, give a toy to a child, paint a portrait, or build our home—establishing our fearless presence by remaining fiercely at ease and arranging our world elegantly.

PART FIVE

LIVING A SKILLFUL LIFE

"And while I stood there I saw more than I can tell and I understood more than I saw; for I was seeing in a sacred manner the shapes of all things in the spirit, and the shape of all shapes as they must live together like one being."
—Black Elk, sacred shaman of the Oglala Lakota Tribe (1863–1950)

The nine slogans in this section explore how to skillfully arrange our lives, world, and livelihood in order to promote fearless wisdom and well-being:

30. Gently bow
31. In a word
32. Join heaven and earth
33. Be a flagpole
34. Don't kick the dog
35. Unseen precise hand
36. Just slow down

37. Take the vajra view of aggression
38. Resonate

When we mix these slogans with our daily life, we engage in a profound conversation with the lively, intelligent world that surrounds us. Instead of recklessly inviting calamities, we shape our experience with exceptional skill. Rather than pointlessly assaulting our world, we instead resolve difficulties and conflicts with inspiration. And instead of fearing life's demands, we master them by embracing each moment with dignity.

30

Gently bow

IMAGINE FOR A MOMENT that everything you see, hear, smell, touch, and taste is your very best friend. The spoon in your hand and the distant sound of traffic; the raindrops running down your back and the smell of dirty laundry; the blue sky and the flavor of cumin—these are not mere passing encounters with two-dimensional items. Instead, imagine for a moment that everything you are experiencing is your very, *very* best friend saying hello.

Such a hello is much more than just a passing handshake or kiss on the cheek. The sky's blue hello invites us to discover something further—something vast and astounding. The smell of an ocean breeze invites us to explore further—to wonder and discover. The sights and sounds around us when fully acknowledged are quite an invitation indeed.

Now, imagine further that we accept our best friend's invitation and say hello back. What would we say and how would we say it?

When we live a fearless life, we return such a gracious greeting by recognizing unmistakably that everything we see, hear, smell, touch, and taste is in fact quite literally our very best friend, and we accept all invitations extended by our very best friend with decorum and great respect: we "gently bow."

On the one hand, bowing is a simple gesture—a human offering—where we extend heartfelt respect toward another. Standing up straight, looking directly at our world, fully appreciating the profound invitation, we acknowledge the remarkable timelessness of it all and we say hello by gently bowing. We actually bow by gently lowering our head in appreciation. This gentleness has no agenda other than to softly open, fully awake to what is fully awake, completely available and exposed. Learning to bow can be a profoundly fulfilling spiritual practice, and for those interested in more formal instruction, I highly recommend receiving guidance from authorized teachers in the lineage of Taizan Maezumi, Roshi.[1]

Such a gesture is not common for Westerners, since many of us tend to think that bowing is somehow demeaning or pathetic, though hundreds of millions of people have been making such a respectful offering for many thousands of years. Despite our hesitations, however, gently bowing out of confidence, as a fearless gesture, is a powerful and subtle spiritual practice that is well worth the effort.

Besides being a gesture of respect, gently bowing is also how we can fearlessly engage our world moment by moment throughout our lives. It is a kind of intelligent, ongoing conversation with our world that is profoundly intimate, filled with paradox and delight, discovery and disappointment. The language that our world prefers for this conversation involves more than words yet is a language nonetheless requiring poise, precision, and openness. In this sense, then, gently bowing is a way of communicating with the sights, sounds, tastes, and smells that surround us, requiring that we become articulate in how we conduct ourselves in our daily lives. We can do this by following three deceptively simple rules:

1. First, do no harm
2. Clean your room
3. Express elegance

First, Do No Harm

When we recognize our world as our very best friend, we may be appalled at how we have been behaving.

- In 2011 human beings destroyed approximately 5,962,000 hectares of forest[2] and dumped 11,227,000 tons of toxic chemicals into the environment.[3]
- Tobacco companies produce 5.5 trillion cigarettes a year— nearly 1,000 for every man, woman, and child on the planet.[4]
- Human beings kill over 50 million animals a year for the fashionable privilege of wearing their skin.[5]

Obviously this is no way to treat a friend, so the very first rule of gently bowing is to avoid doing such things—to do no harm. Now, this doesn't mean that we must troop into the R.J. Reynolds corporate office and accost the executives who are poisoning our world with cigarettes, though confronting them vigorously may be a good idea on occasion. And stopping toxic pollution worldwide is a major enterprise that, for the most part, is not within our immediate control, though we can each play our part in cleaning up, no doubt.

Yet, despite the appalling scale of our collective disrespect toward our very best friend, gently bowing requires that we personally engage our world in a fresh, nonaggressive conversation right here, right now, and that begins with "First, do no harm," which in many respects is quite simple. The gnarly insect crawling up our arm may be distressing, but crushing such a magnificent creature out of convenience is just not how we treat our very best friend. Poisoning our bodies and our world with toxic artificialities may be handy and flamboyant, but it is just not how we treat our very best friend. And recklessly dumping our garbage onto our friend's face—well, we all get the picture, we all understand how to do no harm to our world. "Gently bowing" begins with treating our world as sacred, with the utmost reverence in our every gesture and intent.

Clean Your Room

Once we learn to do no harm, then we must clean our room, literally and figuratively. Cleaning your room should be no problem, really, but it appears that many of us have a tough time of it. Laundry piles up, beds remain unmade, windows get smudged, and kitchens become soiled, and we find ourselves sending a clear message to our world: "Go away—don't come near me." Such a message is the exact opposite of gently bowing.

Cleaning your room has both practical and magical consequences. When we clean our room, we can find our car keys and checkbook. Our kitchen is washed, and dreadful little germs are kept at bay.[6] Our clothing is neatly folded, and when we go out into the world, we are dressed properly. So, as any parent of a teenager knows, cleaning one's room is a sensible approach to living life.

Cleaning our room is not a matter of sterilizing our world, however, where we live in an immaculate, dust-free plastic bowl. Rather, cleaning our room is how we gently bow to our world, inviting our very best friend to play, which involves enormous precision. By literally cleaning our room, we begin to radiate that very same wholesomeness and care everywhere we go—caring for the sights, sounds, and smells around us—which magnetizes a heightened conversation with our world. A kind of mutual dance occurs where we offer care and precision, and our environment responds with insights, gifts, surprises, pranks, teachings, and more. Almost magically, when we respectfully clean our room, our world responds with a profound form of play.

Be Elegant

When we do no harm and clean our room, our very best friend gets the clear message that we are, in fact, friends and would like to have a lifelong conversation. By gently bowing, we treat our world as intelligent and worthy of our respect, and in turn our world playfully responds, and it is through this ongoing play that we learn to gain mastery over our lives.

Normally when we think of mastery, we may envision gaining

power over someone or being superior with a lot of authority. But in the case of gently bowing, mastery is not a matter of dominating or winning but about living a graceful, beautiful life.

If we take a moment to observe ourselves and our fellow human beings, we will notice that we all have an instinct to be elegant. Despite our recklessness and panic, which can often make a mess of things, we all, nonetheless, seek to be beautiful—in small ways, such as how we comb our hair or paint our nails, and in grand ways, such as how we build our homes and invent stylish devices. Such an instinct to be elegant comes vividly alive when we gently bow, and we gain mastery over our lives by being beautiful.

Of course, such mastery is not about becoming a fashion model or a stylish Mediterranean cliff diver. Rather, gently bowing by being elegant is how we confidently sip a glass of water or run a global business—easy, spacious, and firm. Or how we choose to place fresh flowers on our table or serve hundreds of people in our restaurant—gracious, distinctive, and uplifting. Eating raspberries with friends or using an iPad, tending a garden or caring for a sick patient, we master our lives by expressing our delightful elegance in all situations.

Such beauty provokes our world, inspiring nobleness and civility, and we end up in a graceful conversation with our very best friend where elegance provokes elegance, delight provokes delight, and humor provokes humor.

The slogan "Gently bow" challenges us to recognize exactly what is going on in our lives right here, right now, on the spot: the world we live in is not a threat but our very best friend. And if we have the courage to recognize this lively, welcoming wisdom that underlies all that we see, hear, smell, touch, and taste, we will have no option but to gently bow to our world and live a fearless, beautiful life, enjoying the splendid play of it all with our very, *very* best friend.

31

In a word

PICTURE, FOR A MOMENT, a vast ice field sitting atop a mountain peak that each spring melts and cascades fresh water through crevices, down valleys, and into rivers, filling ponds and lakes and nourishing all manner of life. And each winter, snowstorms layer the glacier anew, and in turn, as spring arrives, the ice melts and the process of nourishment begins again.

Such an image, quite familiar throughout the Himalayas, describes the fundamental dynamic of what is traditionally called "mandala" and also describes what I have come to call the Walt Disney Company's "glacier business model."

Let's start with mandala, a common image in Tantric Buddhism; it means literally "circle." Intricately adorned with deities, seed syllables, and various miraculous ornaments, such mandalas are used by meditators to strengthen their visualizations and help realize the fruition of their practice. As maps of the enlightened state, these sacred images offer many profound instructions, and traditionally, it is highly recommended that we receive initiations

from a qualified and realized teacher who can reveal the power and secrets of the mandala. In the case of being fearless at work, however, we will take a more basic approach and acquaint ourselves with how mandala can be understood "in a word."

Essentially, mandala is how everything functions. Whether we are considering a snowflake, a baseball diamond, the human body, or a modern corporation, according to mandala, all express a basic organizing principle that shapes how we and all living beings experience life. Put simply, all mandalas have both a center and a fringe, and such a structure organizes, enriches, and communicates. The center of the mandala is the source of enrichment; the fringe is how it invites, repels, and communicates; and the spacious inner aspect of the mandala is how it organizes. While this may sound strangely theoretical, let's now look at a simple, practical example.

As vice president of human resources at Disney, I often explained to talented recruits how the Disney Corporation worked, calling it "the glacier business model." While "glacier" can at times imply business inertia and weak reflexes, in the case of Disney, it actually describes how the giant global entertainment company functioned as a well-oiled and hugely successful mandala.

At the top of the Disney mountain, established over decades of creative genius and marketing skill, sits a reservoir of widely known and much-loved characters: Winnie the Pooh, Mickey Mouse, Snow White, Peter Pan, Dumbo, and hundreds more. And each year, like clockwork, these characters unfold from the center of the Disney mandala to millions around the world in a highly disciplined distribution ritual touching newborns, children, teens, and adults as theme parks, consumer goods, educational materials, movies, CDs, DVDs, and more. At this "fringe" is Disney's renowned customer service, product quality, and licensing discipline, communicating to millions through its vast array of inviting and entertaining assets.

And each year the "glacier" at the top of the Disney mountain is refreshed with new characters: the Lion King, Buzz Lightyear, Woody, and WALL-E, among others. And each spring, these new characters blend into the cascading refreshment offered to audiences around the world through theme parks, classrooms, movie theaters, computer screens, books—the natural flow of the mandala.

In business, Disney's "glacier" of characters is referred to as the "value proposition," "core business," or "key assets," and managing this "enriching principle" is vital in building a healthy and sustainable enterprise. When we engage mandala as an organizing principle, we seek to understand the core value in its essence: to distill the enriching principle down into a singular potency. Traditionally, the core enriching principle of a mandala can become so concentrated that it is represented as a single syllable, such as *ah* or *hum*.

An exercise I have found helpful when studying and managing organizations is to try to distill its enriching principle in a word: *characters* for Disney, *tax* for the IRS, *capital* for Goldman Sachs, *cure* for Pfizer. Naming the core principle of a mandala in a word is as much poetry as it is commerce, requiring sage insight and finesse. Once named, "in a word" provides a lens for viewing the organization that, depending upon the insight, can reveal, simplify, and instruct; or, poorly chosen, can obscure, complicate, and confuse. So how we recognize and establish the very heart of a mandala can be a helpful skill indeed.

Let's take a very noncontroversial mandala such as religion. Many consider the very core of their religion mandala to be, in a word, *love*. When we experience the basic life force of religion to be love, we produce thousands of men and women around the world extending a gentle hand to millions of people in need of kindness, food, medicine, and support. If, on the other hand, we consider the very core of religion to be, in a word, *righteousness*, for example, we can end up producing dogma, where facts are denied, sectarian bitterness festers, and recrimination turns violent. How we recognize the enriching principle of a mandala can yield very different results indeed.

Let's consider a common American mandala—the baseball

diamond. What is baseball's core enriching principle in a word? If it's *entertainment*, baseball is seen as a source of amusement and fun. If it's *sport*, it becomes how we develop athletically and acquire mastery. As *teamwork*, baseball becomes elegant choreography. Naming the enriching principle in a word, then, can be a lens through which we recognize and establish an organization's basic life force.

While some of us may choose to describe baseball in a word as "sport," "entertainment," or "teamwork"—and each lens surely sheds revealing light on the value of the mandala—for me there is something even more basic about the game that offers an intriguing view into this American ritual: baseball, in a word, is a *mirror*. Here, for decades, America has examined its most prized values of competition, fair play, and teamwork. Here also America has had to confront its most profound shortcomings of racism, hero worship, fraud, and sexism. Throughout thousands of hometowns, families have come together around this mandala to watch their children play, compete, and learn the American lessons of giving your best effort, playing fair, losing with grace, and savoring success. Even today, in the critically acclaimed film *Moneyball*, we once again gaze into our collective mirror of baseball to consider a pressing social challenge: trying to fathom how modern economics and complex computer algorithms shape the simplest of human acts.[1]

When we consider the basic life force of baseball in a word to be a "mirror," we explore America's distilled wisdom, and the sport, entertainment, and teamwork become downstream expressions reflecting who we are as a people.

Of course, there is no "right" answer to what the baseball mandala is "in a word." Nor is there a "correct" single word that captures the basic life force of religion, Disney, or the IRS. Each choice offers a view; each clarifies and instructs to some degree. Each word, no matter which we choose, functions as a lens that brings aspects of the mandala into focus and establishes how we behave in relationship to the mandala. Naming the core enriching principle of any mandala in a word is a matter of insight and skill, requiring poetic play and tough-mindedness.

The slogan "In a word" introduces us to the possibility of grasping the very heart of how an organization functions. While the speed and demand of daily work keeps us focusing on organizing our workplace and deliverables, "In a word" invites us to pause and contemplate exactly how we, our colleagues, and our entire enterprise are in fact enriching the world around us. Whether we are serving drinks at a bar, driving a truck cross-country, or building skyscrapers, "In a word" reminds us that our work is an expression of something powerfully concentrated that informs and drives our efforts, profoundly connecting us to all that we see, hear, and touch. And pausing to understand this power in a word can offer much-needed insight and skill when being fearless at work.

32

Join heaven and earth

I FIRST CAME UPON the phrase "Join heaven and earth" while studying Confucian philosophy in college, and for a time I was clueless about what it meant. Coming from a Christian background, I assumed at first that joining heaven and earth would make my home like God's, as in "Boy, this beer and cigar are great! This is like heaven on earth!" Or maybe the phrase meant that I could pay a visit to heaven, get an early glimpse of the afterlife, and chat with the saints and angels who had all the answers. But after studying a bit, it became clear that joining heaven and earth was about something more profound but nonetheless mysterious. I found that everything from classical Chinese medicine to the oracle *I Ching* to military strategy in Sun Tzu's *The Art of War* was based on joining heaven and earth. One phrase in particular haunted me, over time offering insight into the elegant nature of being human: "The emperor joins heaven and earth."

Words such as *emperor* or *royalty* can conjure up all kinds of negative images, of course. But in the case of joining heaven and

tian (heaven)   *wang* (king)

earth we are not talking about dressing up and playing pretend or ruthlessly oppressing others. Rather, the phrase "The emperor joins heaven and earth" reveals a sacred treasure: human beings are born to express noble majesty. Rather than suggesting a political office, *emperor* speaks to a primal yearning to be dignified.

And rather than referring to cosmic geography, "heaven and earth" speaks to the possibility of fulfilling the greatest of spiritual longings. To *join* heaven and earth, then, is all about becoming fully realized human beings, and traditionally we can do so by expressing the outer, inner, and secret aspects of our royal nature.

Living Life Properly

Understanding the outer aspect of joining heaven and earth is practical and quite straightforward, and it is how we can live life properly. Let's say, for example, that we aspire to be the very best mother or father. We want to give birth to children and raise them well with joy and wisdom. In our hearts we envision loving our

187

children deeply, offering the very best we can offer, inspiring them, protecting them, and sacrificing for them. This noble aspiration to be the very best parent is our "heaven"—our vision of what would be splendid, wholesome, and good.

Yet to be the very best parent, we actually have to give birth to children, which, as some of us know, can be quite messy and difficult. And after giving birth, we have to change diapers, clean bedrooms, check homework, and pay all kinds of bills. For those of us who have had the good fortune to be a mom or dad, we all know the enormity of what is required: endless attention to detail, an eye toward health and safety, and unending energy. This willingness to take on whatever needs our attention is our "earth" as parents—the practicality of shouldering any and all responsibilities.

We express our royal nature when we join our "heaven"—our greatest parental aspirations—with our "earth"—the daily responsibilities of actually being a parent. When we join heaven and earth as parents, we don't just change diapers, we change diapers properly. We make sure we have clean linens and gentle oils to soothe our child's rear end. And we may even sing a little song as we change the diaper, smiling together and feeling fresh and clean as parent and child. "Joining heaven and earth" as we change a diaper requires discipline, joy, and even creativity. When we are joining heaven and earth, even cleaning up the contents of a diaper can be majestic.

This outer aspect of joining heaven and earth applies to just about every human endeavor: running a business, leading a platoon, folding laundry, building a house. As human beings, we have endless possibilities for expressing our noble majesty by blending our greatest aspirations into our most mundane activities. And when we don't—when the emperor does not join heaven and earth—life simply goes astray.

For example, ignoring "earth" can cause enormous chaos. A checkbook unbalanced, a car key misplaced, a monthly report delayed, a phone call not returned—we all know the list and we all know the consequences. On the other hand, when we place some things in "heaven" that don't belong there, such as drugs, money, or fame, we can end up living a fantasy, chasing addictive pleasure, overspending credit cards, and hoping to be someone we are not.

The outer aspect of joining heaven and earth requires that we blend our highest aspirations with life's demands through joy, discipline, and perseverance, and by doing so we learn to live life properly.

Expressing Gentle Presence

Understanding the inner aspect of joining heaven and earth is about being nobly present as a physical human being. This doesn't mean we prance about in brocades or overpriced suits. Nor do we diet to an extreme so we can be seen in public as skinny and desirable. In this case, we are working quite literally with our bodies in space as an expression of having thoroughly trained in mindfulness-awareness meditation. Our head represents heaven, our feet flat on the ground represent earth, and our shoulders and torso are what joins the two.

When we take our posture without joining heaven and earth, we end up expressing our lack of well-being and wakefulness. We may slouch with depression, strut with arrogance, pose out of impoverishment, or stumble cluelessly. In essence, when we don't join heaven and earth, we physically blind ourselves, traveling through, yet out of touch with, life.

On the other hand, when we physically join heaven and earth, we synchronize with the immediate moment and become increasingly familiar with an unmistakable sense of vivid presence that is confident, vibrant, and distinctively gentle.

My teacher, Chögyam Trungpa Rinpoche, went to great lengths to train his students in this inner aspect of joining heaven and earth, instructing us in such principles as "Head and Shoulders," "Keeping Your Seat," "Facing East," "Raising Windhorse" "*Lha, Nyen,* and *Lu*," and much more. He placed such great emphasis on this inner aspect that he established an entire body of martial training to cultivate this bearing of powerful gentle presence. The following is taken from a not widely published 1979 conversation Rinpoche had with his students who were practicing the martial art of the *Dorje Kasung,* or Vajra Guard:

Our approach is very gentle, absolutely gentle, with good head and shoulders and good presence. This is very confusing to people because, in ordinary situations, when we talk about the concept of bodyguard, it means to kill or cure, with bulging muscles. Our approach is that the ladies and gentleman of the Vajra Guard are very impressive and good in their standing, literally speaking. When they open their mouths, when they connect with people, they manifest very gently and beautifully. That's a very interesting kind of weapon, if we could call gentleness a weapon at all. It's a communications system. . . . In our approach to the world the great weapon we have is gentleness. When a person comes to us with doubt or aggression, we, in turn, project our gentleness. If someone can't relate with the gentleness completely, then they begin to realize that behind the gentleness there is also confidence.[1]

The inner aspect of joining heaven and earth requires that we become fully synchronized—head upright, shoulders relaxed, feet on the ground—as a noble, lively presence, and by doing so we naturally manifest a gentleness that cuts through confusion and inspires the best in others.

Being Fully Realized

Understanding the secret aspect of joining heaven and earth requires that we have unshakable confidence in taking the "heaven" view, or what is traditionally called "the Royal View." Taking such a perspective is not a matter of pretending to be an emperor or a queen, nor is it about observing our experience from a lofty place. Rather, taking the royal view is being fully present *as our experience* and in turn discovering that we are profoundly endowed with a natural state of mind that is pure, joyful, and vast.

Taking such a view is not a matter of speculation or wishful thinking, but is an unmistakable intimate experience of our primordial human presence that unfolds from our practice of mindfulness-awareness meditation. Traditionally, such a view is referred to as Mahamudra, or Rigpa, and many of the great masters of the Kagyu and Nyingma traditions went to great lengths to offer students pithy advice in how to realize this "royal view," as is so brilliantly illustrated by the following masters:

191

Longchenpa:

> So stay here, you lucky people,
> Let go and be happy in the natural state.
> Let your complicated life and everyday confusion alone
> And out of quietude, doing nothing, watch the nature
>   of mind.
> This piece of advice is from the bottom of my heart:
> Fully engage in contemplation and understanding is born;
> Cherishing non-attachment and delusion dissolves;
> And forming no agenda at all, reality dawns.
> Whatever occurs, whatever it may be, that itself is the key,
> And without stopping it or nourishing it, in an even flow,
> Freely resting, surrendering to ultimate contemplation,
> In naked pristine purity we reach consummation.[2]

Chögyam Trungpa Rinpoche:

> All aspects of every phenomenon are completely clear
>   and lucid.
> The whole universe is open and unobstructed, everything
> Mutually interpenetrating.
> Since all things are naked, clear and free from
>   obscurations, there is
> Nothing to attain or to realize. The nature of things
>   naturally appears
> And is naturally present in time-transcending awareness.

> The everyday practice is simply to develop a complete acceptance and openness to all situations and emotions and to

all people, experiencing everything totally without mental reservations and blockages, so that one never withdraws or concentrates on oneself.[3]

HH Dudjom Rinpoche:

Although you experience it, you simply cannot describe it— it would be like a dumb man trying to describe his dreams! It is impossible to distinguish between yourself resting in awareness and the awareness you are experiencing. When you rest quite naturally, nakedly, in the boundless state of awareness, all those speedy, pestering thoughts that would not stay quiet even for an instant—all those memories, all those plans that cause you so much trouble—lose their power. They disappear in the spacious, cloudless sky of awareness. They shatter, collapse, vanish. All their strength is lost in awareness. You actually have this awareness within you.[4]

HH Dilgo Khyentse Rinpoche:

Recognizing this gem that exists in us is like finding a hidden treasure that belongs to us under the floor of our own home. It will make us confident that our poverty has been overcome. Resting in that state of recognizing our nature summarizes the dzokchen view. So, we should rest uncontrived in that state.[5]

As these great teachers point out, when we take the "royal view," our "earth," or day-to-day activities, transform from a personal agenda fraught with successes and disappointments, opinions and disagreements, to none other than that very "royal view" itself. Whether we are closing a business deal or scolding a cat, falling in love or swimming a river, our "earth" radiates the very same vivid, joyful, and vast purity that we experience in the "royal view."

Joining heaven and earth, in this case, is about connecting "heaven"—the royal view—with "earth"—the radiant vividness of daily experience—and we do this by becoming more and more familiar with the natural state of mind. The central practice for doing so is mindfulness-awareness meditation, but there are many other practices that great teachers have passed down through the ages that are available to us today. Meeting a qualified teacher who can offer guidance in applying these teachings to our every-day life is highly recommended.

The slogan "Join heaven and earth" reminds us that there is a way to live life fearlessly, with a gentle and regal presence. When we are afraid of our lives, our greatest achievement is to remain safe: to amass joys, ward off disappointments, and keep our heads down to avoid getting caught. But when we join heaven and earth, our greatest achievement is to become a fully realized human being: stepping past our fear, savoring the timeless purity of each moment, and standing up straight, cheerful, and entirely fulfilled in simply being alive.

33

Be a flagpole

IN THE 1990s, as educational publishing was confronting the arrival of technology in the classroom, I was invited by the president of a successful K–12 (kindergarten through twelfth grade) publishing business to help him manage the rapidly unfolding changes. The president, Frank, intended to shift his business away from an editorial-centered approach toward a marketing-driven model designed to adapt to emerging technology, and leading the organization through the change was going to be traumatic and tough.

Working with Frank was truly a joy: he was bright and energetic, and his instincts were unusually astute. Yet he was very protective of his business and was wary of fostering too much change too quickly. After many weeks of planning and analysis, Frank and his staff produced a top-notch change-management plan called "The Future Is Now." Technology trends were reviewed; competitors were assessed; markets were quantified, financials tightened, and time lines set. A central problem loomed, however:

how do we get the forty-person editorial team to relinquish control, embrace technological innovation, and drive the change?

Historically, editorial directors in K–12 publishing set the business pace, keeping in touch with what teachers needed in the classroom and establishing the publishing direction. But with the advent of technology, no one—let alone teachers or editors—could say where education was headed and what the classroom really needed. The desktop computer was becoming the dominant platform, but what about handheld devices and classroom-management systems? Web-based tools were emerging in higher education and surely would trickle down to K–12, but when and how? While editorial leaders focused on the traditional model of classroom education, funds were shifting toward technology, and marketing savvy needed to take the fore.

The sales force—supported with marketing data, new marketing personnel, and consulting expertise—was fast taking the lead engaging teachers, principals, and superintendents in discussing the future of K–12 education, and the editorial staff was beginning to grumble, feeling left out and left behind. The traditional fissures and frustrations between editorial and sales were growing, and we needed to act fast and skillfully.

During a meeting between Frank, the sales vice president, and the three editorial directors, we all mapped out a plan.

"We'll be launching 'The Future Is Now' at our annual sales meeting in two months," the sales VP announced, "and our regional managers are already reviewing the new tools. Of course, there's a lot more to do on product knowledge, samples, demos, and the like, but we are moving along quite well."

"Well, I'm glad to hear you're ready," said one of the editorial directors with a sigh. "Since we are producing the product you are going to sell, maybe you can let us in on how the plan works."

While the tension lingered, another editorial director piped up. "It would be nice to have a launch for our editorial teams, like the sales force gets. Our staff hears a lot about 'The Future Is Now,' but not the specifics. The future may be now for sales, but it keeps being a surprise for us."

Frank glanced my way, and I could see we were thinking the same thought. We had been moving so fast to integrate marketing into the sales force that we had neglected the editorial team.

"Do the editorial staff members ever attend sales meetings?" I asked.

"Too expensive," quipped the sales VP. "We always have the editorial directors there, of course, but flying all those folks down to Sanibel or San Francisco is too much cost and little return."

The editorial directors rolled their eyes.

"Well, maybe we should do something different this year," suggested Frank. "This rollout of the new business model is probably the most important change in our past twenty years, and taking a new approach may be just what we need."

"For my part," I said, "I think inviting all forty editorial staff to attend the sales meeting would send just the right message: that we are all in this together. Plus, we would all know that everyone—sales, marketing, and editorial—had received the same marching orders. I think it would be an excellent team-building opportunity."

"I like it," said Frank with commitment. "Let's plan on having all editorial staff at the meeting and see if we can negotiate some volume pricing on the T and E. Having us all together as we launch, I think, is worth the price."

As the meeting broke up, Frank took me aside. "What do you think? We'll need to course-correct a bit, but I think it will make a fresh start having everyone at the off-site."

As I was about to respond, we overheard the editorial directors talking among themselves as they left the room. "Oh, the fur is going to fly at this meeting," said one director, laughing. "I hope they know what they are getting themselves into."

Frank grimaced and shook his head.

As planning proceeded for the sales meeting, I suggested that I lead a morning discussion among all the editorial staff and the sixty-person sales and marketing team.

"This is a rare opportunity to get this team talking and building rapport," I observed. "I think if we survey all participants prior to the meeting and have a well-managed, open discussion, we could clear the air and quickly create much-needed momentum."

Frank was nervous.

"There will be a lot of old grudges in that room, Michael," Frank fretted, "I think a meeting like that could really get out of hand and do more harm than good."

"Well, if you want to accelerate change and build trust, these grudges have to be surfaced and dealt with," I said encouragingly. "And we'll have everyone in the room at the sales meeting, so from my viewpoint, let's go at it. Managing this kind of change requires candor and leadership, and if there was ever a moment for both, this is it."

"OK," he agreed hesitantly.

When the morning arrived for the large group meeting, we had an added surprise. The chairman of the company had heard about the off-site and wanted to come along too. He was impressed by Frank's business plan and was equally impressed with how Frank intended to launch it at the sales meeting with all the editorial, marketing, and sales force in attendance. Frank had been nervous about the meeting to begin with, but now he was silently having his doubts. Not only were we going to air our dirty laundry, we were now going to do it in front of the chairman of the entire company.

"Maybe we made a mistake planning this free-for-all," he quipped to me over coffee. "The survey returns were not so optimistic, and I'm not sure we should go ahead with this now that the chairman is here."

"Pull the Band-Aid off, Frank," I reassured him. "It will only hurt a bit. Plus, we have nothing to hide. You have a great company that's about to become even better, so cheer up!"

The room was full, with over one hundred people: sales reps, editors, marketing managers, and some people from corporate. Frank stepped to the podium to welcome everyone, especially the chairman.

"Everyone in this room is responsible for building one of the most successful educational publishing businesses ever, educating millions of children in math, science, reading and literature, and much more. We have a lot to be proud of." Frank beamed. "But as we all know, our industry is changing quickly and we need to keep pace, so we are here to launch our new business plan, 'The Future

Is Now.' I am particularly encouraged by having all of you from editorial, marketing, and sales in this room, We don't all get together often, so I want to take advantage of this opportunity."

As Frank introduced me to the group, I could feel his hesitation.

"If we are going to successfully change, embrace technology, and continue to be the leading K–12 publisher, we will need to listen to one another, build new bridges, and work together in new ways. That's why I have asked Michael to bring us through our morning discussion."

I began the discussion with some preliminary observations and some ground rules on giving and receiving feedback: listen openly, be honest and respectful, and appreciate others as they take risks. And we dived in.

"Everyone here was asked to fill out a short survey before today, and over ninety percent of you shared your views, so thank you," I began. "Let's take a look at what we all said."

As I referred to an overhead projector displayed on a large screen, I said, "Here's an item the editorial team addressed: 'I believe the sales force values my opinion on how best to present curriculum and educational materials to the customer.' And how did the editorial team respond? Eight out of ten disagreed or highly disagreed with this statement."

I paused for a moment to let the findings sink in, and I could see Frank squirming as the chairman adjusted his glasses.

"This is a very powerful statement," I said, summarizing. "Eighty percent of us here who make the product for our customer feel that their views are not valued by the people who sell the very same product to the very same customer. Anyone want to clarify this?"

A long silence came over the room, and finally an editor raised her hand. I handed her the microphone.

"I think it's even worse than not being valued," she fumed. "Not one marketing piece has ever included wording, design, or headlines recommended by anyone on our team. We're just flat ignored. I wish the marketing people would stop asking us for our opinion."

Then the floodgates opened.

"Yeah," chimed in another editor, "when was the last time that any of us went on a sales call? Our competitors do it all the time, but not us . . . we're like second-class citizens."

The back-and-forth went on for sixty minutes, and the discussion was contentious and robust. Grievances were aired, opinions were shared, feathers were ruffled, and some voices were raised. And through it all, Frank sat up straight, clearly on edge as the chairman occasionally wrote a note or leaned over to share a remark.

"OK, let's take a break," I announced to the group. "This has been a powerful discussion, and we'll pick it up again in twenty minutes."

As the group slowly left the room to refresh their coffee and make some business calls, Frank took me aside out of earshot and he was panicked.

"This is a disaster, Michael, and this discussion is ruining my company!" he fumed with clenched teeth. "The results of the survey say that we're not a team, people are pissed off, and no one trusts each other. And now you're opening this whole thing up— in front of my boss, no less—and making matters worse."

Frank paced.

"Let me ask you a question, Frank," I interrupted. "What do you think the team needs from you right now?"

"They need me to get control of this and get the genie back in the bottle!" he bristled.

"What they need from you right now, Frank, is for you to lead," I spoke pointedly. "And that means *be a flagpole!*"

"A 'flagpole'? What is that supposed to mean?" he asked.

"Look, your organization is disoriented and off its game right now. You know it, they know it, and the numbers in our survey show it. The organization has to face its confusion, sort it out, and resolve issues, and that's exactly what they're doing this morning. But when they look to you, they need to know it's all right. They need to have something they can look to that orients them, that lets them know that despite the difficulties and confusion, they are moving in the right direction. They need a flagpole, Frank, and you are it."

He began to calm down.

"You've asked your people to take a risk today, and they have. They are speaking their minds openly and honestly for the first time in a long time. And to do that in front of you and your boss takes courage, and that means they trust you. You're their flagpole; you are what they can look to, letting them know that they can take risks, speak their minds, and confront difficulties. This is how it feels to lead, Frank, and instead of panicking, may I suggest that you take note of what you see."

I led him out toward the coffee line.

"What do you see, Frank?" I asked. "Take a good look at your people and tell me what you see."

We both surveyed the room. People were animated, talking,

and laughing. We noticed editors speaking with sales reps; marketing specialists sharing coffee with editors; and two sales managers chatting intently with an editorial director. The chairman was sitting with several sales reps and two editors, talking, nodding, and listening.

"I don't know about you, Frank, but to me this looks like a success so far. Your people are moving, right before your eyes, past the grudges and disappointments, and they are actually acting like the team you need: speaking their minds, listening to one another, trying to sort out the future. All you have to do is just sit there and be a flagpole—which is exactly what they need. It may not be easy, but it is simple."

For a moment Frank paused to soak in his team and what I had said. And as if on cue, the chairman ambled over to us and asked, "So how do you think it's going, Frank? People sure seemed fired up."

Frank looked at me for a moment and smiled. "I think they're doing great. It takes a lot of courage for them to speak their minds, and I give them all a lot of credit."

The team spent the rest of the morning processing the survey results, meeting in smaller groups, and planning for future collaboration. There were some tough conversations, but with them came some insights and understanding. And when Frank brought the group together in order to close, he asked, "What did we learn this morning? Anyone want to sum this up?"

After a few people offered some final remarks, a young sales rep stood up.

"I joined this company from one of our main competitors two

months ago. I'd heard so much about what a great publishing house this was, but I never *really* knew until today. This meeting took a lot of guts—nobody runs meetings like this. We all got a true picture of one another today. We didn't just go over slide decks and business plans; we told each other the truth, and I, for one, want to thank you, Frank, for having the confidence in us to have this discussion. I learned more this morning about my team than I could have in years of meetings and telephone calls. We've got a long way to go, but I am looking forward to doing it with this team."

While no one applauded or cheered after the new sales rep's short speech, there was a quiet, shared recognition among many that they had taken an important step that morning. And sure enough, they all went on, under Frank's guidance, to successfully execute their "The Future Is Now" business plan, publishing award-winning programs that led the way in bringing technology into the K–12 classrooms.

The slogan "Be a flagpole" reminds us that leadership is not always moving forward, getting it done, and driving for results. Sometimes it requires us to stop and simply *be*—often in the midst of the most difficult circumstances. Such a gesture can orient those pressed by daily demands and reassure those willing to step out and take a risk. And if we were to pause and "be a flagpole" for a moment, we may notice that by simply stopping we are showing confidence in our colleagues and getting a truly wide view of how to be fearless at work.

34

Don't kick the dog

COLLECTING EMOTIONAL TROPHIES at work can be a disastrous preoccupation. We may *think* that we are working to complete the project on time, make the sale, or close the deal. But when we look closer, we often find that we want the satisfaction of triumph, the reassurance of recognition, and the pleasure of bragging rights. While succeeding can be fun and gratifying, no doubt, too often it's about pointless emotionality.

Collecting such emotional trophies can often be petty, like "confidentially" discussing a colleague's inadequacies, reminding others of our credentials, or conspicuously displaying our wealth. When such cheap emotionality becomes monumental, we can create vast suffering and disaster, as witnessed in American political discourse or the multibillion-dollar divorce industry.

Fortunately, we can tame such cowardice by learning not to "kick the dog."

In one of my assignments, I supported a biotech physician, Mandy, who had the challenge of merging teams of medical and scientific affairs advisors and researchers. The business was under financial strain, and the goal was to build a leaner, more focused team while maintaining working relationships with key opinion leaders. On paper the plan and the new structure looked great: small teams were aligned by therapeutic area, populated with both physicians and pharmacologists, and organized to support the commercial product leaders. Mandy was smart and well respected, and she was quite skillful in maneuvering corporate politics. However, her boss, Arthur, also an MD, held a grudge common to many physicians: when it comes to medical advice and research, those in medical affairs with an MD after their names were the experts, and the PhDs in scientific affairs—chemists, pharmacologists, toxicologists, and the like—should play a supporting role.

Needless to say, Arthur's perspective would not prove helpful in merging the two departments, and Mandy worked hard to keep her manager in line while she cultivated respect and collaboration between the two organizations. Despite her best efforts, however, she could not completely restrain Arthur's impulse to condescend and collect emotional trophies, which proved disastrous.

As the date neared for the launch of the reorganization, more and more communications flowed outlining who would report to whom, how product leads would consult with various scientific experts, and what marketplace institutions aligned with each team. And despite a few bumps along the way, the restructuring was going well, until Arthur distributed an e-mail that derailed the entire project. The memo read well for the first three or four paragraphs, recognizing people's hard work and offering reassurances. And then in the final paragraph, Mandy's boss felt a need to write:

I am quite confident that our new structure will help us meet our budget goals, but more importantly we will now be organized to strengthen our physician-to-physician dialogue in the marketplace, for it is our physicians' hands-on experience with patients that truly distinguishes us in the marketplace. So, congratulations on your hard work, and I look forward to working with all of you in making our new organization a success.

When Mandy and I read the e-mail, we were speechless. After months of helping the organization build trust and shed old habits, her boss was able, in one fell swoop, to remind everyone that physicians remained the experts in the new organization and that all others were second-class citizens. As the calls poured in from angry scientists, Mandy invited me to have lunch with her and Arthur.

"Boy, it seems that a lot of people got the wrong impression from my e-mail," Arthur remarked innocently as we finally got around to the topic.

"Wrong impression? What impression *were* you trying to make?" I probed.

"Well, since the restructuring was going to kick off next week, I just wanted to thank everyone and recognize their hard work." Arthur responded, with an innocence that seemed slightly feigned.

"But why didn't you let me see the e-mail first, the way you do all other e-mails that you've sent out about the restructuring?" Mandy asked, jumping in with an edge in her voice. "And why did you have to end with such a stupid remark implying that physicians were more important in the marketplace?"

Arthur was wide-eyed, and my client was at her wit's end.

"I have to say, I agree with Mandy," I joined in. "The e-mail read quite nicely until the end, where it seemed like you needed to remind everyone that you, Mandy, and all the other MDs have the upper hand—"

"I don't see it that way," Arthur interrupted.

"Then why does everyone else see it that way?" responded Mandy. "I have received at least twelve phone calls, dozens of e-mails, and now, here you sit with me, the person in charge of the restructuring, along with the consultant, and we, like everyone else, see it that way. Look, you've already sent the message and everyone got it, I'm just wondering why you felt a need to do this!"

The atmosphere was tense, but Mandy had called it perfectly.

"Well, if I have created problems, I'm sorry," Arthur responded genuinely. "Throughout this restructuring I have noticed that many people on the scientific affairs team spoke of the restructuring as if they were going have the same voice in the marketplace as physicians, and you both know there are concerns there. Physicians want to hear from physicians, and I just feel that we don't have to pretend about that—"

"Pretend about it! Pretend about it!" Mandy barked. "You know as well as I do that this is the most sensitive issue we had to manage and that I have worked very hard at it, so who's pretending, for God's sake?"

"You had to go and kick the dog, Arthur," I summarized, nodding my head.

"What dog?" he asked as he and Mandy looked at me like I was nuts.

"Look, what you and Mandy are trying to do by merging medical and scientific affairs is a very delicate leadership challenge. It takes patience and nuance. It's like skillfully walking through a city neighborhood of homes, backyards, and patios without causing any commotion or alarm. It's a very sensitive proposition. In the same way, it's very tricky walking around the emotional territory of these scientists and physicians. They are very aware of signals concerning position, rank, and status, and Mandy has maneuvered quite successfully. And to her credit, most everybody has begun to put their sensitivities aside and has been working well together. So, at last, all the neighborhood dogs have been lounging or resting, and if they've noticed us walking by, they at least haven't barked or strained at their chains. But you, Arthur, had to kick one of the dogs. You had to remind everyone that the status of physicians is one step above. So I have two questions for you: What happens when you kick a dog in a city neighborhood? And why would someone kick a dog in the first place?"

Arthur and Mandy had dropped their confused stares but were still a bit perplexed.

"Well, when you kick a dog in a city neighborhood," I continued, "he begins to bark, but more importantly all the other neighborhood dogs begin to bark as well. And right now we have a lot of barking scientists, that's for sure. And the challenge we face is no longer the important business of successfully restructuring the department; the challenge now is dealing with the barking. By your kicking the dog we have lost focus and instead we are now trying to manage emotional mayhem.

"And why would someone kick a dog at all?" I asked. "Well, I can tell you that when I was a kid, I would never kick a dog, it wasn't in me. But I had friends that did, and they kicked a dog for only one reason: it made them feel emotionally superior. They would antagonize a dog on a chain and feel an emotional jolt for just a moment, like getting a useless little trophy."

"I never kicked dogs when I was kid," said Mandy with a smile.

"Neither did I," chimed in Arthur sheepishly.

"Well, we definitely have that in common." I laughed.

Arthur, Mandy, and I finished our conversation, and Arthur admitted that he may have gotten a little emotional satisfaction out of including that final line in the e-mail. But unfortunately, from that point forward the restructuring did not go well. Trust was in short supply, frustrations were worn openly, and physicians and scientists worked at cross-purposes. The e-mail was referred to often, and both Arthur and Mandy moved on to other jobs.

The slogan "Don't kick the dog" reminds us that we can pay a heavy price when we choose petty emotional victories over fearlessness. As with our physician friend, Arthur, such emotional victory can seem satisfying in the moment, but it inevitably leads to wider "barking" and useless emotionality. Especially when others are depending on us to build rapport in risky situations, to foster respect among many stakeholders, or to be a fair broker in conflict, "Don't kick the dog" is a sobering reminder of our responsibility to be confident, trustworthy, and authentic. When we engage circumstances skillfully, we respect sensitivities, acknowledge boundaries, and build trust—there is no need to taunt or savor easy triumphs. In the end, "Don't kick the dog" is all about emotional confidence when circumstances demand skill rather than cowardice.

35

Unseen precise hand

WE ALL WANT to be a hero, on occasion, fearlessly engaging life's injustices: righting a wrong, rescuing a distressed friend, confronting a bully. Starting at an early age, all of us at some point imagine ourselves as noble and heroic, and such aspirations are what make us human beings so utterly lovable and dignified.

Being a hero has its problems, however. In our earnestness to rescue others, we may find ourselves making a bigger mess.[1] Like a Don Quixote, we could end up pursuing a well-intentioned crusade to make people's lives better but end up leaving a trail of misery and anger.

Or in our effort to be helpful and heroic, we may impulsively jump into difficulties unprepared, like leaping into a river to rescue a distressed friend only to recall that we can't swim. Being fearless in the face of life's cruelty and threats requires much more than mere earnestness. Such fearlessness demands well-honed precision, flawless timing, and emotional wisdom, and we can access such skill by practicing the "unseen precise hand."

During the 1970s and '80s many of the people who were study-ing Buddhism in New York City also trained in a martial art. For my part, I studied Okinawan Karate Zen for two years and I was miserable at it. I never got past white belt, and I could barely re-member, let alone flawlessly execute, the *katas*—the elegant cho-reography of the art. But my teacher, a true warrior sage, was very generous, and after our workout and *zazen* meditation session, we would repair to the local tavern, where he would offer dharma instruction over glasses of beer. As you can imagine, I very much enjoyed studying with this wise Zen teacher.

Of course, unlike myself, there were many Buddhists who ex-celled at martial training, and one of them was a friend, Maria, who over the years mastered Tai Chi and became quite a teacher herself. One evening after Maria had delivered a stirring dharma talk, she began to demonstrate the soothing, yet formidable dance of Tai Chi, at one point appearing almost to turn in mid-air while balancing on one foot. As she completed her instruc-tion, students asked questions. "Where did you learn such an art?" "How can Tai Chi blend with Buddhist meditation?" "What is Chi?"

Finally, one student asked, "Did you ever use your marital art on the street?" and Maria paused, smiled, and said, "Yes, in fact, I have . . . but only once, in a New York subway station."

I could hear a story coming and I was prepared for a classic "against-all-odds" heroic encounter where Maria would confront a bully and dramatically save the day. Yet, at the student's request, Maria recalled an encounter that proved to be far more elegant than the one I had expected, because it demonstrated the princi-ple of the "unseen precise hand."

"It was evening, around eight, and I was on the local Number One train on my way downtown to visit a friend," she began. "By the time I reached my station, there were few people left in the subway car, and as I exited, I began to climb the stairs to the street, alone.

"As I rounded the corner on the steps toward the next flight of stairs, I was suddenly confronted by a man from out of the shadows, who had cleverly positioned himself in a blind corner where he could observe and then surprise his victim. He was within eight feet of me and was moving to close the distance, when I instinctively took my posture, prepared to instantly defend myself. But right there on the spot he paused, and in that split second our eyes met, and he knew full well that one more step forward would have been fatal. As he backed off into the shadows, I lingered for a few seconds, attentive to his presence, and then slowly resumed my climb to the street."

I, for one, was mesmerized by Maria's story but a bit disappointed by the lack of climax. I wanted a bit more drama—a literal "punch" line—and little did I know, I was about to get one.

"As I climbed the final flight of stairs," Maria continued, "I noticed a young girl descending, unaware of the danger lingering two flights below, and as I passed her—"

Maria stopped, stepped toward a student, and gently illustrated a flowing movement of her hand that turned the student easily about.

"—I placed my two fingers on her elbow and lightly turned her to accompany me up and out of the subway. Without a word between us, hand on her elbow, I escorted her to the intersection and toward a different stairwell, and then suggested, 'Why don't you try that subway entrance instead? I think that would be a bet-ter choice.'

"As I removed my hand from her elbow, the young girl became confused as she reoriented herself and began to question, 'What happened? Where am I? What's going on?' 'Everything's fine . . . just fine,' I said. 'I think you'll be safer taking that entrance,' I again suggested. I smiled a bit and then went on my way.

"And so, as you can see," Maria concluded, "Tai Chi can be re-ally helpful in just getting around town!" We all laughed in silent appreciation.

As I pondered Maria's story later that night, I realized that I had wanted her to create a scene of furious conquest, a story that would have provided an aggressive thrill rather than clarify true fearlessness. And it is right here, in this yearning for reckless en-tertainment, that we can understand the lesson of the "unseen precise hand."

In order to be truly heroic and to gain victory over fear and aggression, we must exhaust our need for petty satisfaction and instead cultivate an utterly precise and clear way of being in the world. Whether we practice the martial arts or oncology, zazen or business leadership, ikebana or computer science, mastering our particular discipline is vital, for it provides a form for being in the world—a foundation from which to skillfully act. When we wholeheartedly commit to being our form—whether martial, ar-tistic, business, or otherwise—we grow confident in our discipline and way of life, and we can find ourselves succeeding almost ef-fortlessly without a need to demonstrate our prowess or savor the tasty recognition.

In Maria's case, she had taken her training to heart and mastered the discipline of Tai Chi, and she had the capacity to act with tremendous precision. And because she instinctively valued skill over thrill, she had no need to create a scene, remaining emotionally invisible yet in command.

Such a lesson applies to more than just rescuing neighbors from thugs. In business, as well, there are all kinds of hidden shadows and lurking adversaries that require that we master our livelihood skills and offer an "unseen precise hand." Just as we wouldn't combat a thug without martial training, so in business we wouldn't unmask a fraud without legal precision or confront a toxic leader without immaculate political jujitsu. Demanding clear accountability, questioning a sugarcoated sales pitch, challenging financial deception, resolving a festering competitive grudge—the list is familiar and long—requires not only our noble aspirations but, more important, a fearless presence that can execute flawlessly and with perfect timing: clear-cut, without emotionality; skillful, without creating a scene.

36

Just slow down

I AM OFTEN INVITED to speak at universities about how mindfulness-awareness meditation might help promote health and wellbeing within higher education. I am honored by the many invitations and equally impressed with the singular challenge that so many universities face: in our speed to succeed, students, faculty, and staff more often than not find themselves feeling under siege.

I have experienced this "siege mentality" quite viscerally when I visit some campuses. I recall leading a weekly meditation class at a top liberal arts college. The students who were attending the sessions were clearly some of the brightest of the bright: passionate, insightful, and hardworking.

However, the learning atmosphere seemed to radiate an unspoken sense of panic. For example, everyone seemed to be on the verge of doing "something else"—some responsibility loomed large and impending; whether it was homework, a project, a paper, or a meeting, each student seemed to be "rushing" through his or her life rather than actually living it. Our discussions after our meditation sessions were often about the relentless pressure to succeed, excel, and demonstrate mastery. As one student put it, "When you take the top one or two graduates from the very best high schools and put them all in the same room and set unrealistic expectations, this is what you get: high-achievers competing with high-achievers who feel pressure from all sides. Many of us just burn out."

Apparently this "siege mentality" is widespread:

- "Record Level of Stress Found in College Freshmen," a front-page *New York Times* article, reported that the emotional health of college freshmen had hit a twenty-five-year low. While a greater number of students saw their emotional health taking a nosedive, "their drive to achieve and their academic abilities were trending upward."[1]
- *Race to Nowhere*, a widely popular independent film, documents the enormous pressure high-schoolers endure in seeking a college education. The film reveals a "silent epidemic in our schools: cheating has become commonplace, students have become disengaged, stress-related illness, depression, and burnout are rampant, and young people arrive at college and the workplace unprepared and uninspired."[2]
- According to the University of Illinois Wellness Center, about one out of three college freshmen report feeling "overwhelmed." And this is in a nation where suicide is the second leading cause of death in college populations.[3]

217

This is not to say that attending college should be a leisurely walk in the park. Striving to get a 4.0 average or to compete for the very best internship can be an inspiring and brisk adventure indeed. But why the "siege" with all the rush, anxiety, and burnout? In the case of many universities, the problem may be systemic.

In very simple terms, universities organize themselves around four "communities": faculty, administration, students, and governance. And these four communities are expected to work together to promote learning and advance society. While I may be oversimplifying it, such an arrangement is nonetheless common to most universities.

When engaging the daily work of education, however, many universities confront a distressing fact of life: faculty, students, administration, and governance tend to act like isolated "silos" rather than coordinated communities.[4] "Silos" are not unique to universities, of course. Institutions of all kinds are challenged with isolation-prone subdivisions, and inspiring "silos" to step beyond their boundaries is a perennial leadership challenge.

In universities, however, isolated departments, communities, even individuals can be unusually rigid and in turn unintentionally foster a siege mentality. Faculty members, pressured to "publish or perish," often consider student demands as distractions and administrators as obstacles. Students, expected to graduate with excellent grades—often as quickly and inexpensively as possible—frequently see faculty and administration as roadblocks, not supports. Administrators, expected to enforce policy and provide quality service, often experience their student and faculty "customers" as adversaries, not as colleagues. "Silos," pursuing their own interests rather than supporting one another, increasingly treat others as roadblocks, obstacles, and even threats, and the pressure of a siege builds.

Now, there are countless professors and students who share delightful rapport, and thousands of administrators who are inspired and collaborative, no doubt. The challenge is in creating a healthy and nurturing climate, in a system that pressures for achievement while unintentionally encouraging conflicting goals. Many professors, administrators, and students know how it feels when confronted with such a system: ordinary problems blossom into threats, conflicts amplify into insults, and a siege mentality becomes institutionalized where we feel compelled to protect ourselves from our vocation rather than actually fulfill it.

Revitalizing such a stressful atmosphere, whether in a university or in any institution, is a major leadership challenge requiring superior management and innovative teamwork. But to get to the root of the problem—to gently release the siege mentality—requires a very simple gesture: to *just slow down.*

Slowing down at universities isn't as strange as it may sound.

- Harry R. Lewis, dean of Harvard College, sent out an acceptance letter to incoming freshmen entitled "SLOW DOWN: Getting More Out of Harvard by Doing Less," which counseled, "[By] slowing down . . . you are more likely to sustain the intense effort needed to accomplish first-rate work in one area if you allow yourself some leisure time, some recreation, some time for solitude."

- Maurice Holt, professor of education at the University of Colorado, in his paper "It's Time to Start the Slow School Movement," suggests, "Is this the time to start the slow school movement? I believe it is an idea whose time has come . . . slow schools give scope for invention and response to cultural change, while fast schools just turn out the same old burgers."
- Justin Broglie, after experiencing suicidal depression in his freshman year of college, started the Mindful Revolution, "a student-run initiative at the University of Pennsylvania exploring how mindfulness, positive psychology, and character development can transform our education system from the inside out."

The sanity of "Just slow down" reaches far beyond universities, of course, and can be applied to many aspects of living a fearless life. In fact, "just slow down" is a movement that has spread throughout the world. Beginning in Rome in 1986, the slow movement started in reaction to the opening of a McDonald's hamburger fast-food franchise, when a journalist, Carlo Petrini, asked a simple question: "If there's fast food, why not slow food?" which in turn blossomed into an international movement to just slow down. Today Petrini's simple question has generated Slow Food, Slow Parenting, Slow Gardening, Slow Money, Slow Travel, and yes, Slow Education in over 132 countries.[5]

The slogan "Just slow down" reminds us that slowing down—whether at school, at work, or in life in general—is a fearless gesture because it requires us to stop anxiously running from, past, and to our experience. By slowing down we can stop feeling inconvenienced or threatened by the raw demands of our lives. We touch rather than rush. Savor rather than gulp. Study rather than cram. And in the process, we confidently step out of our siege mentality into a richer, more human experience.

37

Take the vajra view of aggression

PEOPLE CAN BE remarkably aggressive toward one another. And just to be clear, we are talking about you and me—not just the other 6,976,280,148 people on the planet.

At one extreme, we can be aggressive in petty ways, such as cluelessly reaching into the group popcorn bag after sneezing into our hand, or gossiping about a neighbor's failure. At the other extreme, we can be inconceivably cruel and ruthless, bullying the weak or torturing and murdering one another with hideous passion. When we take a true measure of how we mistreat one another as human beings, it's hard not to collapse in tears and melt away. But when living a fearless life, melting away is not an option, and instead of collapsing in despair we can learn to skillfully work with human cowardice by taking the vajra view of aggression.

Taking such a view starts with recognizing who's attacking whom, which may appear pretty straightforward: people attack people. Simple enough. Day in and day out, we insult one another as marauders and cheats, bullies and bandits, betrayers and sociopaths.

Yet upon closer examination, we may find that life's threats and insults are not so clear-cut. In fact, human aggression seems to be free-floating, moving about fluid and shapeless. One minute our new boss is an inspiration, the next she is impetuously firing us. One day we are in love, the next we are in divorce court. One year we are supporting the mujahideen, the next they are bombing our cities. When we take the vajra view, we recognize aggression to be this moving paradox, a human gesture born out of fear and confusion—a pattern of obnoxiousness that is fickle yet deceptively convincing. Taking the vajra view of aggression requires that we appreciate this adaptive resilience of aggression and avoid the tendency to form a fixed, self-serving view.

Once we recognize the challenge to be aggression and not other people, we then must unmask our own aggression: How do *we* expose others to ridicule or harm? When do *we* condescend? How tall is *our* arrogant stance? Such self-reflection is not an exercise in disparaging ourselves, but it is how we stop blinding ourselves from seeing aggression clearly. By recognizing our own cowardice, we can stop amplifying mere insults into threats, inconveniences into disputes, misunderstandings into lawsuits, and in turn get a true measure of the problem. To take the vajra view of aggression, we need to step past our own cowardice so we can directly engage the raw distastefulness of the world's insults, which, needless to say, requires tremendous bravery.

When we are willing to open to aggression, we not only taste the full flavor of the misery, we also notice that the insult is a window into the other's heart, and there we can get a clear picture of what we are dealing with. When we fearlessly open to aggression rather than be repulsed, we can directly experience its adaptive power. We can see the wisdom within the confusion. I remember learning this lesson firsthand from my son, Hayden, who at the early age of six took the vajra view and peered through the window of my aggression.

During a dinner party, I and a friend got into a heated argument over a perceived injustice supposedly delivered by a third party upon a mutual acquaintance. As is my personal style of obnoxiousness, I argued my case angrily but persuasively, presenting a hard and fixed view that the offending party should be banished! Exiled! Scorned! In the midst of the argument my son walked up to my friend, who at this point was clearly frustrated with my posturing, and quietly observed, "When my dad gets angry, his wisdom looks really silly." Needless to say, I was stopped in my tracks, and my friend got a good laugh. But I always recall my son's insight as perfectly illustrating how to take the vajra view of aggression.

Rather than buying into and arguing with my obnoxiousness, my son peered through it to see how my intelligence was being intoxicated by my anger. My son didn't freeze me into a fixed view as a simple idiot or pompous loudmouth—that would have been easy enough. He saw my aggression, but more important, he saw how it had hijacked what he typically experienced as a healthy and intelligent father. He looked through the window of my insults and saw the wisdom within the confusion.

From this vantage point, taking the vajra view of aggression is not about cataloguing the foulness or depravity of other people, which, frankly, is not that hard to do. Taking the vajra view of ag-

gression is about recognizing how human wisdom and dignity get misdirected, distorted, and hijacked into cowardly, obnoxious behavior. It's easy to catalog Dick Cheney's many leadership failures, but understanding how his fierce patriotism and extraordinary management prowess were transformed into ham-handed arrogance is a subtle challenge indeed. Stanley O'Neal, a former CEO of Merrill Lynch, was a greedy, arrogant, self-absorbed leader who was voted one of the worst American CEOs of all time. The hard part is understanding how O'Neal's remarkable intelligence and well-honed management skills were so alarmingly misdirected. Osama bin Laden was a vicious mass murderer, no doubt, but how did such a pious, devoted man became so shockingly insane?

Traditionally, taking this view of aggression is likened to throwing a vajra, or thunderbolt, at confusion in order to transform it into wisdom. This stylized tantric ritual object, commonly used in Vajrayana Buddhist practices, displays four or eight sharp prongs surrounding a spike, all of which pass through a lotus into a central orb. Ideally made of meteoric iron, the vajra is considered the ultimate indestructible weapon that, when thrown at the enemy, pierces to the heart and grabs hold of the enemy's confusion—the hatred, callowness, and cruelty. And as the vajra's razor-sharp prongs hold the enemy's confusion, the central spike penetrates to the enemy's core and, touching the inherent wisdom in the confusion, permits such health to glide down the spike, through the lotus, and into the orb. Then, by command, the vajra returns to the hand from which it was thrown, delivering the essential insight into what compels the enemy's aggression.

I am not suggesting, of course, that we go to the local Tantric Yoga bodega and stock up on vajras so we can go about tossing them at our enemies—though there have been masters in the past who have tossed a few at their obnoxious students, I am sure. Taking the vajra view of aggression, however, is about getting to the heart of the matter, not just marveling at people's aggression, and the vajra provides us a perfect weapon for doing so, because the only way to hold and throw a vajra is to be completely fearless—utterly free of arrogance and willing to completely touch the crude, juicy, and foul aspects of what makes human life so confusing and painful.

When we are willing to take the vajra view of aggression in this way, we can discern what needs to be nourished and what needs to be confronted. We have the option of building trust or building a boundary, offering a soothing remark or offering a sharp rebuke. Because we are not afraid of our experience, we are willing to taste the squalor of it all while seeing the problem clearly. By taking the vajra view of aggression, we are no longer singularly impressed by the pettiness or depravity, but more curious and inviting of the entire display and willing to more skillfully engage the seeming threat.

The slogan "Take the vajra view of aggression" reminds us that we can be fearlessly curious about human obnoxiousness despite its foul odor and creepiness. Rather than being blinded by the insult, we can peer directly through it and in turn clearly see the wisdom behind the aggression, and by doing so we have the choice to lend a hand, get out of the way, or end the confusion altogether.

38

Resonate

IN MY ROLE as an executive coach, I often work with leaders who have difficulty building support for their ideas and priorities. Especially in complex organizations, such as pharmaceuticals and universities, leaders can often become disoriented by the political landscape, where diverse stakeholders compete for shrinking resources and allegiances are fluid. Yet in all cases, my clients can point to someone in their organizations who has mastered the politics and garnered support for their ideas. And while much distinguishes those who can successfully maneuver in these complex settings, a prominent characteristic is their ability to "resonate."

In his best-selling book *Social Intelligence: The Revolutionary New Science of Human Relationships*, Daniel Goleman goes beyond his prior work on emotional intelligence to "lift the curtain on an emerging science, one that almost daily reveals startling insights into our interpersonal world. The most fundamental revelation of this new discipline is: we are wired to connect."[1]

On the one hand, such a discovery seems pretty obvious. We all fall in love; we all get angry with one another on occasion. We not only connect with one another, we also connect with cats, parrots, trees, and even space aliens. So recognizing that we human beings are "wired to connect" is, well, kind of stating the obvious, like "water is wet" and "things move around."

But what is so powerful about Goleman's study is that we are more than simply wired to connect. In the words of Daniel Stern, MD, a research psychiatrist at the University of Geneva, "our nervous systems are constructed to be captured by the nervous systems of others, so that we can experience others *as if* from within their own skin, as well as from within our own."[2] In short, we are not just wired to connect, we can *resonate*—experience the "other" intimately, directly, and unmistakably.

Stern investigates this human capacity for directly knowing the other in his book, *The Present Moment in Psychotherapy and Everyday Life*, where he painstakingly documents through clinical observation and interviews how we as human beings permeate each other's presence. While Stern's fascinating work concentrates mainly on the relationship between patient and analyst, his findings shed profound light on our everyday experience, where we can often find ourselves living a "shared feeling voyage . . . where two people travel together in the present moment through a similar landscape of feeling where shifts in feelings serve as landmarks," which includes "a mutual recognition of making this voyage together . . . an inter-subjective phenomenon."[3]

Resonating with another so directly and so personally is not just limited to those we love or to familiar settings. In fact, experiencing another person's heart, mind, and feelings directly and unmistakably can and does happen to all of us all the time—if we just slow down and notice.

Many years ago I had the misfortune of rupturing disks in my spine and was laid up in bed for several weeks recuperating. As my convalescence progressed, I would, on occasion, take a short walk outside my apartment on the Upper West Side of Manhattan. Cane in hand and feeling fragile, I would slowly—very slowly—shuffle around my block, gradually regaining strength in my back and legs. As a six-foot-two-inch Irishman, I was used to feeling invincible, and this injury was my first experience of being physically vulnerable, and facing such a reality was both an emotional test and a spiritual adventure.

On one of my daily shuffles around the block, I noticed an old woman in her late seventies shuffling down the sidewalk directly toward me, cane in hand. It was mid-afternoon, the sun was shining on a cloudless autumn day, and few people were about; we could clearly see each other as we slowly—*very slowly*—converged on each other. We each had ten long minutes to contemplate our meeting—like mirror images, wounded, frail, and hobbled, though also so different: a strong Irishman and a frail old woman. And as we closed the space between us and slowly passed each other, our eyes met, and right there on the spot I knew her unmistakably and I knew she knew me the same. She was glad to know that she was not alone with her frailness and was relieved to see that even the strong could understand. And I could feel the lonely helplessness of growing old for the very first time, and I was happy to lighten her load for just a moment. For that moment we shared a voyage—I knew she felt my heart, and I felt hers—we had resonated.

Needless to say, experiencing such resonance is a profound human ability, and confidently "experiencing others from within their skin" at work can make all the difference in the world when it comes to creating a dignified, inspiring workplace.

On one assignment, my client, an experienced research scientist sporting both an MD and a PhD, constantly found himself at odds with his commercial and operational colleagues on how best to bring a promising surgical device through late-stage clinical development. Arrogant, impatient, and unable to "resonate," my client was often out of touch with his colleagues and in particular a toxicologist who felt diminished and disrespected by his rudeness. "She is incompetent and in over her head," he would often remark. "She should stop pretending to be a physician and stick to her knitting."

After several months of coaching, my client and I had a breakthrough conversation:

"How did your meeting go with the toxicologist yesterday?" I asked.

"I am trying my best and I think I am getting better," he responded, trying to recollect positively his attempts at being more collaborative and less rude.

"Did you notice anything new about her? Anything that you may have overlooked in the past?" I probed.

"Not really," he hesitated. "She continues to keep a tight control over things and she did seem a bit tired."

"A bit tired . . . how so?" I pushed.

"I don't know, like she was maybe sad or something?" he intuited.

"Like her heart is broken?" I gently suggested.

And for a moment my client paused and, with a sudden glance of recognition, understood what it felt to " experience others from within their skin."

"You are right," he softly recollected. "She is sad . . . why I don't know . . . and I had never seen it before. I guess she really is more complex than I noticed . . . and she kind of touched me. . . . It feels like this is the first time that I have actually seen her!"

"And what you may not know," I gently informed my client, "is that she has recently divorced and is now a single mom of two small kids."

As my client slowly looked up, we both paused and glimpsed each other—*resonant* and relieved.

Like so many of us at work, my client had blindly cut himself off from his colleagues. He had dulled his natural ability to resonate and experience others from within their skin. Yet, through self-reflection and hard work, my client was able to revitalize his instincts to touch others directly, and he continued to develop, becoming attuned and open to his colleagues and more skillful in building alliances.

The ability to "resonate" is crucial at work, whether we are seeking to retain talent, make a sale, assess a problem, or successfully innovate. As reported in an article in the *Harvard Business Review*, "Finding and Grooming Breakthrough Innovators," the authors' research found that the defining skill of great organizational innovators is *resonating*—appreciating the hearts and minds of others:

Innovators must be able to walk into a conference room full of diverse constituents, including colleagues, customers, subordinates, bosses, vendors, and partners, and quickly discern the underlying motivation of each one. They leverage that information to craft and communicate a message that resonates with every constituent. This is the art of bringing a diverse group onto the same page—and it is absolutely essential to transforming an interesting idea into a company-wide innovation.[4]

Resonating with our world and those around us, whether in a business meeting or just walking down a city street, is how we live life fearlessly, and we can learn to reawaken this ability to resonate by practicing mindfulness-awareness meditation.

When we sit on a meditation cushion for hours, weeks, and years, we eventually discover a simple and dynamic fact: *our mind is perpetually curious.* Not in the sense that we are constantly searching for a treasure or an insight to a problem, though such curiosity arises, no doubt. Rather, the curiosity that we rediscover through mindfulness-awareness meditation is a creative, agile awareness—a soft, pliable, yet sharply alert fascination with our immediate circumstances. Whatever our situation offers, be it hot or cold, pleasant or irritating, inviting or repulsive, we discover that our minds are fearlessly inquisitive and willing to resonate with whatever occurs. Traditionally this form of resonant wisdom arising out of meditation is likened to a child's delight, a parent's loving attention, or a tiger's curiosity. By dropping our arrogance and fear through training the mind in meditation, we attune ourselves to our immediate circumstances and discover that we are, by our very nature, intimately curious and in touch with our world.

Traditionally, our ability to resonate and experience others from within their skin requires a fearless commitment to four existential immediacies of being alive: nowness, egolessness, openness, and noble decorum.

Nowness

The singular unavoidable and undeniably penetrating reality that we face is "nowness." Through the practice of mindfulness-awareness meditation we awaken to this vivid, raw immediacy that is ungraspable, yet inviting us to touch and be touched. Only in nowness can we resonate with others; "now" is when we live our lives—everything else is some form of rehearsal.

Egolessness

When we cultivate awareness in meditation, we let go of tracking experience from the view of "me" and "mine," "yours" and "theirs." Through such "egolessness" we become aware that the whole situation resonates, interweaving "me," "others," "activities," and "communications" as a vibrant cloth. There is no particular object of awareness or any scorekeeper. Instead, we find that we are authentically curious as the situation brings us along.

Openness

By sitting still in meditation for long periods, we inevitably open, free to touch the situation completely on its terms. Such openness is an expression of a fearless trust in our experience and in ourselves. Just as a water bowl reflects the moon, we resonate with our world, utterly impartial and completely available.

Noble Decorum

To resonate with our world and with those around us is to express a form of "cosmic courtesy" where we instinctively respect our world as sacred. We have given up on our complaints and aggression and we no longer speed past our experience as inconvenient nor rush toward the tasty bits to make us happy. We treat every aspect of our world with impeccable manners. Traditionally, such noble decorum is referred to as "One Taste"—resonating completely with each and every experience that presents itself.

The slogan "Resonate" encourages us to totally and completely open to our world and recognize such openness to be ultimately compassionate. We are wired to connect, able to experience others from within their skin—if we have the courage and gentleness to do so.

ACKNOWLEDGMENTS

Writing this book was a joy and a challenge, and many friends supported my efforts. With deep appreciation, I want to thank the Shambhala team for its support, kindness, and discipline: Beth Frankl, Ben Gleason, Jade Weston, Julie Saidenberg, Jennifer Campaniolo, Hazel Bercholz, Daia Gerson, Jonathan Green, Sam Bercholz, Sara Bercholz, Leonard Jacobs, Ashley Goodwin, John Golebiewski, and Nikko Odiseos. I extend a warm and firm smile to the many good friends who offered their wisdom: John Brown, Susanna Lack, Stephanie Tade, Ralph Jaffe, Jeremiah Fruchtman, Judy Hirsch, Doug Axelrod, Ellie Byrom-Haley, Trish Broderick, Don Barr, David Nichtern, Doug Barasch, Alex Devaron, Matt DiRodio, Susan Piver-Browne, Libby Weathers, Patton Hyman, Mark Hurwich, David Sable, James Gimian, Barry Boyce, Yi Yuan Tang, Steve Hove, Doug Lindner, David Huehner, and Kira Jacobs. And, of course, I want to extend my deepest love and gratitude to my parents, Thomas and Elaine Carroll, and my teachers, Dudjom Rinpoche, Trungpa Rinpoche, and Sakyong Mipham Rinpoche—without their kindness, all would have been lost.

APPENDIX A

Cultivating Fearlessness through
Shiné-Lhagtong *Meditation*

Shiné-lhagtong meditation—commonly referred to as mindfulness-awareness meditation—is a practice that is fundamental to the Kagyu-Nyingma tradition of Tibetan Buddhism and literally means "calm abiding, clear seeing." When we practice *shiné-lhagtong* meditation, we learn to tame our restless mind, recognize our inherent wakefulness, open gently toward others, and ultimately live a fully realized, fearless life. Such a discipline is a lifelong practice requiring skill, perseverance, and humor, and receiving regular face-to-face guidance from a qualified teacher is highly recommended. Generally speaking, the practice unfolds along four broad guidelines:

Motivation: *Fearlessly opening to whatever occurs*
Mindfulness: *Vigorously training attention*

Awareness: *Becoming familiar with primordial presence*
Relaxing: *Resting thoroughly*

Motivation—Fearlessly Opening to Whatever Occurs

Science has been documenting many of the benefits of practicing mindfulness-awareness meditation. For example, with only short amounts of practice, we can grow the part of the brain that regulates our emotions,[1] and with sustained practice over months we can significantly revitalize our immune system.[2] Or with a daily practice we can gradually improve our emotional intelligence and sense of well-being.[3] Over the centuries, accomplished practitioners of mindfulness-awareness have spoken of many intriguing paranormal benefits, such as clairvoyance, mastery over the elements, and divination. But while these benefits are inspiring, no doubt, engaging the practice properly requires that we eventually drop our desire to achieve any benefit whatsoever and instead resolve ourselves to perfecting a very simple yet demanding gesture: *fearlessly opening to whatever occurs.*

Such an undertaking seems straightforward enough, but opening to whatever occurs becomes increasingly subtle and demanding as we practice more and more. At first, we quite reasonably may come to meditation motivated to relieve our personal suffering or confusion. Or maybe we have read about becoming wise, joyful, and healthy through meditation and would like to become such a person. Over time, however, practicing mindfulness-awareness reveals that accomplishing *any* ambition is questionable, and we notice that practicing teaches us to *discover* rather than achieve and to *recognize* rather than accomplish.

Shedding our motivation to achieve takes time and humility, through which we slowly soften to ourselves and to our lives. Rather than aspiring to become someone else—someone who is less confused and a healthier version of "me"—we instead slow down, ease up, and begin to notice who we are. This demands that we *open*—making ourselves utterly available to anything and everything that occurs. Whether we are sitting on a meditation cushion or parking a truck, studying a rare wisdom text or sewing up a wound, our motivation becomes to fearlessly open to whatever occurs.

Traditionally such openness—such willingness to be entirely available to our world without any preconditions[4]—is considered the core gesture of compassion, and this becomes not only our motivation for practicing mindfulness-awareness but also how we increasingly recognize who we are and how to behave in the world.

It is vital, therefore, that our motives for practicing mindfulness-awareness permit us to engage our experience authentically. And this is why the motivation we are traditionally encouraged to cultivate is compassion, or the willingness to fearlessly open to whatever occurs.

Mindfulness—Vigorously Training Attention

In some sense, the *shiné*, or mindfulness, aspect of meditation is an artificial exercise where we sit still for long periods in order to sustain our attention on an object. Essentially, mindfulness is about remembering to bring our attention back to whatever is occurring. It's kind of like going to the gym to work out rather than just naturally swimming in the ocean or walking up a mountain. We very deliberately work out: noticing where our attention is, intentionally escorting it to an object, and working to sustain our attention on that object. Such training can be very monotonous and exquisitely demanding, requiring alertness, vigilance, and precision.

In mindfulness-awareness, sustained attention is not so much a goal of the practice, but more how we recognize that we can stop rehearsing our lives and instead live them directly in the immediate moment. Such sustained attention, while a natural expression of the mindfulness-awareness discipline, is not, however, sufficient for learning to live a fully realized, fearless life.

For many of us, when we come to the practice, we would like to calm our minds and experience a little bit of *shiné*, or calm abiding. And, typically, we struggle, trying to make our busy minds behave themselves. Using the mindfulness technique, we recognize where our attention is, notice our thoughts, and bring our attention back to our breath or an object. When we vigorously train our attention in this way, an ironic shift eventually occurs. Rather than seeking calmness in the busy display of our mind, we notice that our mind is already naturally calm in *how we notice* the display. We shift from trying to make our minds behave themselves to abiding calmly *as a mind* that is noticing itself.

Such a discovery shifts the practice, and over time our attention stabilizes and we become one-pointed—calm, clear, and attentive to whatever arises. Mindfully and calmly abiding in this way, we open further to our experience and become sharply curious about our circumstances.

Awareness—Becoming Familiar with Primordial Presence

Typically, we experience meditation and our lives in general as what is traditionally called a dualistic situation—"me over here" encountering "that over there"—which is natural enough. There is a lot of stuff "over there" that we need to attend to: picnic tables and sharp knives, hurricanes and fast traffic that need our attention. But in *lhagtong,* or awareness meditation, we realize that such a dualistic perspective is a narrow window that, while giving the impression as complete and accurate, is, in reality, a confined and partial view of a much larger and accessible perspective—a *primordial presence.* Recognizing this larger presence is *lhagtong,* or clear seeing, and we do this in the practice in three ways:

- Synchronizing
- Analyzing
- Glimpsing

Synchronizing

Through the discipline of calm abiding we eventually notice that our mind, body, and world are not unfolding as three separate and seemingly uncoordinated aspects of life—in other words, our dualistic situation—but instead we recognize that we are intimately woven together—mind, body, and world—as a primary immediacy, an undifferentiated physical nowness, which we experience in the meditation and in everyday life as our synchronized presence.

Analyzing

The more familiar we become with being a synchronized presence in nowness, the more we become curious about what exactly is going on here. For example, it is not unusual for *lhagtong* practitioners to seek answers to questions such as "Where is this 'mind' that I am trying to observe in meditation?" "What is a 'thought' and where does it come from?" "Since I can only experience 'now,' where is the past and why is the present ungraspable?" Traditionally, shaping and training the mind's natural curiosity as it seeks to investigate its synchronized presence is of the utmost importance, and the Kagyu Mahamudra tradition offers many excellent instructions for examining this nondual nature of mind.[5]

Traditionally, engaging Mahamudra instruction is done only under the guidance of a qualified teacher who is capable of giving what is called "direct pointing-out instruction." Such instruction is vital because "direct pointing out" is how the practitioner unmistakably and clearly recognizes what is, in fact, going on here: the truth that our synchronized presence is unbiased, timeless, and vast—a primordially pure state of mind—and we have ready access to this pure awake presence because, despite our seeming confusion, it is exactly how we have been experiencing our lives all along.

Glimpsing

When we mingle our calm abiding with our primordial synchronized presence, our meditation shifts further from the artificial checking of attention to "just being primordially present." Practicing in this way is subtle and demanding as we become more and more familiar with being fearlessly awake *as* primordial presence rather than striving to do so. We may struggle to extend our experience of this wakefulness or try to recall how best to enliven the experience, but such strategies prove useless, and we discover that becoming familiar with primordial presence is about *glimpsing*. Whether during brief moments or extended episodes, by surprise or through deliberate technique, the practice of *lhagtong* teaches us how to recognize this sudden and vivid arising of our natural state of mind, and over time we become familiar with being primordially present.

Relaxing—Resting Thoroughly

The more familiar we become with calmly abiding as a primordial presence, the more confidently we live a fearless and simplified life, free of the mistaken complexities of being a coward. Rather than picking and choosing our experiences, trying to hoard life's pleasures and ward off life's difficulties, we instead discover that we can taste all of life's encounters deeply and thoroughly, with a full and vigorous presence. Here our meditation shifts even further from synchronizing, analyzing, and glimpsing to *relaxing*. Such relaxing is not about sitting by the pool and reading a comic book, though this is not excluded, of course. Rather, relaxing, in this case, is how we become increasingly familiar with how timeless, all-pervading wakefulness discloses every experience—good, bad, happy, or sad—as primordially pure, and it is from this sacred outlook that we confidently express our primordial presence and live a fearless, realized life. Traditionally, it is highly recommended that we practice in extended solitary retreats under the guidance of a realized teacher in order to fully appreciate this discipline of relaxing and resting thoroughly.

Finally, at some point in the practice of mindfulness-awareness, circumstances definitively shift, and we discover that we are effortlessly and irreversibly awake. Many inspiring stories of Buddhist masters recount this shift: Tilopa slapping Naropa with his sandal,[6] Bankei observing his own spittle while lying on his deathbed,[7] Mahakasyapa[8] smiling during Shakyamuni's flower sermon. For those who practice mindfulness-awareness with great effort and devotion, such a shift occurs as a profound irony, as if we had mistakenly been living our lives backward, walking in reverse, observing our world as it recedes. For suddenly, we discover, almost by chance, that we were perfectly designed to live our lives moving forward—facing ahead as we walk, going toward our experience rather than away from it. And we simply wake up to a natural rhythm that we possessed all along but had misunderstood and overlooked. Like rediscovering how to walk, finally, we wake up unmistakably and irreversibly—fearlessly at ease—and at this stage of meditation, there is really nothing to do but rest thoroughly and walk forward.

APPENDIX B

Instructions for Mindfulness-Awareness Meditation

Posture

When we practice mindfulness-awareness meditation, or what is commonly called "sitting meditation," we take a posture sitting upright, relaxed and alert. Our eyes are open, with a soft gaze; our hands are placed palms down, gently resting on our thighs. Our chin is tucked in and our gaze is slightly downward. Our face and jaw are relaxed and our mouth is slightly open. We breathe normally and sit still. If we are sitting on the floor, on a cushion, our legs are loosely crossed. Or we may choose to sit in a chair with our feet firmly on the ground. Under all circumstances our posture remains the same: upright, precise, and relaxed.

Thinking and Labeling

When we "sit," we have two distinct experiences. First, we notice the simple vividness of our immediate circumstances: the faint sound of passing traffic, the color of our rug, the gentle pressure of our hands on our thighs, the soft smell of incense. Our senses are sharply alive, and our experience in the immediate moment becomes uncomplicated and simple.

Second, we also notice that we are thinking: talking to ourselves, commenting on this and that, thinking about any number of things. Particularly if we are sitting for the first time, we may find ourselves unusually restless with our thoughts. Such restlessness is not a problem; it is what we work with in sitting.

Attending to these two experiences—being alert in the immediate moment and thinking—is central to sitting practice, and working with them properly requires a precise yet gentle awareness of the breath. The next instruction for sitting meditation, then, is that when we notice ourselves thinking, we label our thinking by silently saying "thinking," and then we bring our attention gently to our out-breath. In effect, we label the thought "thinking" and bring our attention back to now.

Attending to the Breath

Attending to the out-breath in such a way requires patience and vigilance. Particularly at the beginning, we may find our minds wandering and rarely attending to our out-breath. By persevering in the practice, however, the mind gradually releases its fascination with ruminating and, instead, calmly witnesses whatever arises.

By resting with the out-breath, we find that we can keep our attention on our out-breath just as if we were gently running our hand over a piece of silk. Slowly, precisely, again and again, we gently place our attention on our out-breath, and eventually we find balance where we are both mindful of our breath *and* mindful in the immediate moment.

Attending to the out-breath is not just a mental tracking of the breath, however, where we attempt to concentrate and "observe" our breath. Rather, we attend to our breath by physically *feeling* the breath as it moves. Our attention is a physical attending, riding the bodily movement of the breath: the moving of our chest, the sensing of the breath across our lips, the sound of our breath, and the feeling as it leaves our nostrils. Attending to our breath is about living the physical immediacy of breathing rather than mentally tracking the experience.

In this style of mindfulness-awareness meditation, we place our attention only on the out-breath and permit our in-breath to function without any deliberate attending. By practicing in this way, we experience a distinct "gap" in our practice, where our attention is left with no object of meditation for a brief moment at the end of each breath. This gap at first can be disorienting or feel a bit spacey, but over time, by mindfully attending only to the out-breath and letting the in-breath be, we discover that we are opening to and through the gap, expanding our practice beyond the mechanics of training the attention to synchronizing our presence with the vivid, immediate space around us. This synchronized presence heightens the emphasis on the awareness aspect of the meditation.

General Remarks

The meditation instruction presented here is called mindfulness-awareness, or sitting meditation, and it comes from the Tibetan Kagyu-Nyingma Buddhist tradition. This instruction is enough to get you started, and it could even be all you'll ever need. But most likely this will not be the case. As you go further with your daily meditation practice, questions and obstacles will arise, which is quite natural. Traditionally, it is recommended that meditators receive face-to-face instructions from another person qualified to teach mindfulness-awareness meditation. This way you can appreciate the instruction, examine what is expected, and ask questions. For a list of locations where you can receive meditation instruction, please go to my website, www.awakeatwork.net.

Generally, you will want to cultivate a regular sitting practice, keeping to a schedule each day. At first, fifteen minutes in the morning or evening will be ample time, but gradually you will want to extend your practice, sitting thirty, forty, or perhaps sixty minutes a day. But it's important to begin where you can, not to force yourself. You can extend the time of your sitting period naturally rather than feeling pushed or obliged. It is recommended that you set aside an area in which to meditate, uncluttered and free from distractions. Choosing to buy a meditation cushion and other accessories is fine, but sitting on a chair or stool is fine as well.

The instructions given here are deceptively simple, so I encourage you to take your time and work with them gradually and wholeheartedly.

APPENDIX C

*How Mindfulness-Awareness Cultivates
Social Intelligence*

Work is all about mastery, where we demonstrate how to make stuff happen. Whether we are computer engineers or bartenders, neuroscientists or welders, engaging our world and bringing about preferred results is how we contribute to building a human society.

Such mastery is more than just making our world behave itself, however. We may think, at times, that being technically proficient is adequate, but we soon discover that work and life demand more—that we must execute both flawlessly and skillfully, properly orchestrating the larger stage of human relationships that support our efforts. And when such relationships are not properly attended to, they can grow toxic and dysfunctional, frustrating our best efforts to get the job done.

Mastering our job requires a broader intelligence, where we not only ensure quality but also inspire others to feel pride in doing so; where we not only make a profit but also protect others and take risks responsibly; where we not only make the sale and close the deal but also build respect and camaraderie along the way. Mastery of our job, then, is about demonstrating our technical skills flawlessly while skillfully cultivating the healthy human relationships that make mastery possible.

In his best-selling book *Social Intelligence: The Revolutionary New Science of Human Relationships* Daniel Goleman maps out seven skills for cultivating the healthy human relationships that are vital to mastering work and life in general. And, not surprisingly, his study finds that we are built to be skillful with one another, that our "brain demands that we be wise" in shaping and being shaped by each other's emotions and biology, and that we are hardwired to instinctively harmonize with one another.

But such instincts can grow weak and fallow if we take them for granted. Especially if we permit the numbing effect of anxiety, aggression, and fear to dull our social intelligence, we can find ourselves frustrated with work rather than mastering it, oppressed by life rather than inspired by it. And one way to strengthen our natural ability to form healthy human relationships is through the practice of mindfulness-awareness meditation.

At first glance such a proposition may appear absurd: by sitting still for long periods of time we can become more socially intelligent and skillful. But despite the seeming counterintuitive disconnect, this is one of the many exquisite ironies of practicing mindfulness-awareness meditation, and below is a brief outline detailing how mindfulness-awareness can help cultivate the eight social-intelligence competencies described in Goleman's study.

Primal Empathy

Goleman's definition: feeling with others; sensing nonverbal emotional cues.[1]

"The ready ability to sense the emotions of another. A low-road capacity (neuro-circuitry that operates beneath our awareness), this variety of empathy occurs—or fails to—rapidly and automatically."[2]

How Meditation Helps Cultivate This Capacity

One of the outcomes of practicing mindfulness-awareness meditation over many years is a decided shift from "mentally" tracking our experience as a "removed presence"—which can distance us from our spontaneity through commenting on, rehearsing, or worrying about scenarios—to being in prolonged, direct somatic contact with the present moment. Such awareness, where we are "synchronized" with our experience versus "removed" from it, permits spontaneous access to our somatic expressions. Such self-awareness unfolds differently for each practitioner, sometimes marked by initial awkwardness, forced "noticing," or wildness that steadily gives rise to a confident awareness of unspoken somatic and social cues.

Attunement

Goleman's definition: listening with full receptivity; attuning to a person.[3]

"Attention that goes beyond momentary empathy to a full,

sustained presence that facilitates rapport. We offer a person our total attention and listen fully. We seek to understand the other person rather than just making our own point."[4]

How Meditation Helps Cultivate This Capacity

Typically, we listen to others through the filter of a "mind-set." If we are looking for a business deal or a romantic relationship, we listen for social cues that will guide us to determine the likelihood of making a deal or striking up a rewarding connection. While relying on mind-sets in order to discern is not a problem, being *unaware* of doing so is. Through extended mindfulness-awareness meditation we learn to recognize how mind-sets influence our outlook, agilely drop the mind-sets when necessary, and in turn bring our unbiased attention to the immediate moment.

Such attention is not merely a noting or observing, however, but a highly sensitive openness, requiring confidence to be fully exposed to our immediate experience.[5] This attunement that unfolds from mindfulness-awareness is broader than Goleman's "offer[ing] a person our total attention and listen[ing] fully," since through the practice we open to a conversation with the entire phenomenal world, attuning not just to the social cues but to the play of an organic intelligence beyond animate and inanimate.

Empathic Accuracy

Goleman's definition: understanding another person's thoughts, feelings, and intentions.[6]

"Builds on primal empathy but adds an explicit understanding of what someone else feels and thinks . . . bringing high-road circuitry (neuro-circuitry that operates more methodically and with deliberate effort) to the primal empathy of the low."[7]

How Meditation Helps Cultivate This Capacity

Through mindfulness-awareness, we familiarize ourselves with our own intimacies: sitting silently for long periods, we get to know ourselves up close and personal, and gradually we stop feeling impoverished, harsh, or arrogant about our various unique features. Such intimate familiarity with ourselves unfolds as a "gentleness" that naturally probes and appreciates others' emotional presence. Traditionally, how such gentleness is expressed by mindfulness-awareness practitioners is referred to as "the four immeasurables":

- Loving-kindness—recognizing another's happiness and working to cultivate such happiness on their behalf.
- Compassion—recognizing another's suffering and working to relieve them of such suffering.
- Sympathetic joy—recognizing and delighting in another's joy.
- Equanimity—being equally curious toward all concerning their well-being.

How accurate mindfulness-awareness practitioners are when recognizing another's thoughts, feelings, or intentions is traditionally treated as a phenomenological issue versus a quantifiable event, which can include such abilities as glimpsing clearly, directly introducing, softly touching, mutually opening, jointly knowing, and more.

Social Cognition

Goleman's definition: knowing how the social world works.[8]

"Know what is expected in most any social situation . . . adept at semiotics, decoding social signals."[9]

How Meditation Helps Cultivate This Capacity

Another outcome of practicing mindfulness-awareness for prolonged periods is that we free up our cognitive function from anxiously keeping score of our experience. Typically, we expend tremendous amounts of mental and emotional energy trying to determine if we are being treated fairly by life: Are we being insulted, cheated, disrespected? Are we being loved, recognized, appreciated? Such "emotional scorecarding" becomes increasingly pointless for mindfulness-awareness practitioners, and this frees up our natural curiosity, which had been forced to play scorekeeper. Such curiosity, traditionally called *prajna*, or "supreme direct knowing," is highly attuned to whatever unfolds, taking a fresh, almost childlike interest in the unique contours of experience.

Prajna is traditionally considered the wisdom with which the practitioner glimpses and ultimately rests with the primordially pure state of enlightenment, engaging all situations—social and otherwise—as a resilient, spontaneous direct knowing.

Synchrony

Goleman's definition: interacting smoothly at the nonverbal level.[10]

"Lets us glide gracefully through a nonverbal dance with another person. . . . Getting in synch demands that we both read nonverbal cues instantaneously and act on them smoothly—without having to think about it."[11]

How Meditation Helps Cultivate This Capacity

Another outcome of practicing mindfulness-awareness for extended periods is what is called "dancing with the phenomenal world." While such a phrase may sound a bit soft and self-indulgent, it nonetheless speaks to a broader sense of synchrony, where the practitioner recognizes the fluid insubstantiality of experience and, rather than resisting, generously embraces life's flowing momentum. Such an ease of being unfolds into the practitioner's social setting and beyond. Whether it's the grief of losing a loved one or the passion of falling in love, the exquisite relief of sitting by the ocean or the grueling effort of climbing a ridge, mindfulness-awareness practitioners learn that "gliding gracefully" with the unspoken momentum of it all is how we confidently open to our experience and taste it completely on its own terms.

Self-Presentation

Goleman's definition: presenting oneself effectively.[12]

"The ability to 'control and mask' the expression of emotions is sometimes considered key to self-presentation. People adept in such control are self-confident in just about any social situation, possessed of savoir faire."[13]

How Meditation Helps Cultivate This Capacity

Mindfulness-awareness practitioners place a primary emphasis on learning *how to be* over learning *what to do*. We may want to become a fantastic portrait painter or a brilliant CEO, to play the violin or run a marathon, but for mindfulness-awareness practitioners we must first resolve a fundamental issue: can we be at ease with who we are under all circumstances? Resolving such a core issue is not a matter of cheerleading our way through life's difficulties or keeping a stiff upper lip as we face life's many unknowns. For mindfulness-awareness practitioners, answering such a question is the visceral essence of the practice where we unmistakably reconnect with an inherent confidence that affirms that we are completely capable of "being" on this planet. Such confidence unfolds from mindfulness-awareness into social situations as poise[14] that is not so much controlled as it is relaxed, not masking emotions but agilely expressing them.

Influence

Goleman's definition: shaping the outcomes of social interactions.[15]

"Expressing ourselves in a way that produces a desired social effect like putting someone at ease. Artfully expressive people are viewed by others as confident and likable and in general make favorable impressions."[16]

How Meditation Helps Cultivate This Capacity

Another outcome from practicing mindfulness-awareness over prolonged periods is the development of what is traditionally called *upaya*, or skillful means. Essentially, skillful means is caring for what needs care, accommodating what needs accommodating, discarding what needs to be discarded. In short, upaya is doing whatever is needed to bring about wakefulness and well-being for others. Such skillfulness in shaping relationships and outcomes springs directly from the wisdom of prajna, or supreme direct knowing, where we see clearly the other person without any filters or mind-sets.

Typically, because we experience people through our mind-sets rather than directly as who they are, we undercut our attempts at influencing or lending a hand because we end up influencing imaginary people rather than the actual people themselves. But after prolonged mindfulness-awareness practice, we increasingly drop this tendency to relate to imaginary people, and instead we see the other clearly, with no filters. Such exposure can be disturbing for those involved, since such interactions are based on vulnerability, so they require courage and humility.[17]

In the end, the upaya developed out of mindfulness-awareness is an emotional agility that shapes human exchanges as they fluidly unfold, promoting health, sanity and well-being.

Concern

Goleman's definition: caring about others' needs and acting accordingly.[18]

"In the world of work, concern that propels us to take responsibility for what needs doing translates into good organizational citizenship. Concerned people are those most willing to take the time and make the effort to help out a colleague."[19]

How Meditation Helps Cultivate This Capacity

It does not take long for mindfulness-awareness practitioners to discover that to be human is to be tender. Sitting alone on a cushion for extended periods readily reveals this simple, ordinary, human softness. Too often we can find ourselves covering up our tenderness, however, by putting on a Botoxed face, curling up in a ball, or lashing out in anger when touched by life. When we practice mindfulness-awareness, we find that such a struggle is self-defeating and instead recognize that our tenderness is, in fact, human wisdom that inclines to be expressed. Such tenderness moves us to care for ourselves and others—to show genuine concern—and we discover that our tender vulnerability is powerful, and that as humans we are built to be decent, kind, and helpful to others.[20]

APPENDIX D

Four Fearless Traditions

Kagyu-Nyingma Meditative Disciplines

The meditation practices referred to in this book originate from the Kagyu and Nyingma lineages of Tibetan Buddhism, drawing specifically upon the contemplative practice of *shiné-lhagtong,* or calm-abiding/clear-seeing. Many of us in the West may be familiar with aspects of this tradition under the popular heading of "meditation" or "mindfulness," and nowadays various forms of mindfulness meditation are being taught at universities, hospitals, and places of business around the world. These Kagyu-Nyingma meditation practices uniquely emphasize a direct and unmistakable familiarity with our inherent wakefulness as the very ground of meditative discipline. Such training is indispensable, since it shows us how to directly explore our fear and in turn recognize how such distress introduces the possibility of living a fearless, enlightened life. Traditionally, it is recommended that practitioners receive instruction in the practice of *shiné-lhagtong* from an authorized teacher. For those interested in receiving direct instruction, please contact my website, www.awakeatwork.net.

Shambhala Warrior Practices

In the mid 1970s, Chögyam Trungpa Rinpoche[1] presented a body of teachings called Shambhala Training. Many Tibetan masters—especially the Sixteenth Karmapa,[2] the spiritual leader of the Kagyu lineage; and Dilgo Khyentse Rinpoche,[3] the spiritual leader of the Nyingma lineage—recognized these teachings as fulfilling the legendary vision of the Kingdom of Shambhala.[4] While there are many practical and profound methods involved with these Warrior practices, at their very core, these teachings introduce the practitioner to a simple yet remarkably powerful fact of life: by embracing fear at its most fundamental level, we can rediscover a primordially pure way of living that is unspeakably awake, formidable, and utterly at ease. Many Shambhala Warrior, practices are drawn on throughout the book, and for those interested in training in the sacred path of the Shambhala Warrior, please contact Shambhala International at www.shambhala.org/shambhala-training.php.

Sun Tzu's Military Principles

The Art of War, as it is popularly known in the West, is a classic Chinese military text attributed to a late-sixth-century B.C.E. military general named Sun Tzu. While many have learned to wage war from the text, some Buddhist practitioners have learned to apply the principles in order to skillfully work with conflict and discord *without* resorting to aggression or violence. By blending the skillful principles of the Sun Tzu with the practice of *shiné-lhagtong*, the practitioner can realize a profound and at times almost magical ability to command circumstances, providing a kind of spiritual agility that can resolve conflict precisely and compassionately. Accessing Sun Tzu's principles can be quite challenging, however, and the translation and academic commentary by James Gimian, Barry Boyce, and the Denma Translation Group[5] can provide excellent guidance in more formally training in the wisdom of Sun Tzu.

Kasung-Command Protection Methods

Typically, working with conflict, aggression, or shock is not considered particularly spiritual or even practical. Living a fearless life, however, requires that we work directly with such powerful forces, and to do so, Tibetan Buddhists traditionally practiced protector disciplines such as the four-armed Mahakala.[6] In order to bring these traditional protection principles alive in a modern-day setting, Chögyam Trungpa Rinpoche established the Dorje Kasung practice—literally, "indestructible command protection"—which provided his students a path for skillfully working with the most demanding and troublesome aspects of being human.

There are few references to the term *Kasung* in traditional Tibetan texts, but in the memoirs of Tulku Urgyen Rinpoche the great Dzogchen master speaks of *terdag*, a "spirit who is entrusted with the terma's [hidden secret teachings] safekeeping." The memoir goes on to describe these terdag in the following way:

> Such a guardian is often called a *kasung*, a guardian of the teachings. The highest type of guardian is known as a *ying-kyi kasung*, "guardian of the dharmadhatu teachings," which includes such protectors of the male and female classes as Ekajati and Damchen Dorje Lekpa.[7]

The practices of the Dorje Kasung, as taught by Chögyam Trungpa Rinpoche, are multifaceted. They include encamping in remote areas, overseeing the safety and well-being of the Buddhist community, providing personal security to teachers, learning military and martial disciplines, establishing a well-organized and uplifted atmosphere for presenting Vajrayana teachings, and mastering communications techniques that promote authenticity and decorum. While the Dorje Kasung practices are generally not publicly available, for those interested in learning more, see the limited edition of *True Command: The Teachings of the Dorje Kasung*, by Chögyam Trungpa (Halifax, Nova Scotia: Trident Publications, 2003) or contact Shambhala International, www .shambhala.org/kasung.php.

APPENDIX E

Instructions for Contemplating the
Fearless at Work Slogans

By deliberately reflecting on life's delights, challenges, and paradoxes, we can slow the turbulence of our mind and allow our innate wisdom to guide us. Like permitting cloudy water to rest and gradually become clear, contemplation eases our daily speed and stress, gently allowing the dignified confidence of *ziji* to shine.

1. Choose a peaceful setting: You may choose to stroll along a wooded path, sit quietly in a shrine room or church, or simply have a cup of tea at your kitchen table. Basically, choose a physical setting that is soothing and calm.

2. Be mindful: Take a moment to let go of the inner dialogue and appreciate the immediate surroundings. Simply notice the sights

and sounds, appreciate the quiet openness of the moment. Practice mindfulness-awareness meditation for three to five minutes.

3. Recall the purpose: We do not contemplate in order to gratify our hopes or dispel our fears. By contemplating life's circumstances we are expressing our confidence that it is worthy to consider decent, skillful ways to conduct our lives and be helpful to others. Try contemplating this short verse:

> Without hope and without fear
> May I be decent in my actions;
> May I be helpful to others.

4. Invite and consider the object of contemplation: Read a particular slogan. Let the mind and heart freely and curiously consider the ideas and images that come to mind: recall experiences; explore the perspective that is provoked; feel excitement, curiosity, sadness, or distress thoroughly. Note any emotions and physical feelings that accompany the topic and write down any particularly helpful ideas or suggestions that come to mind. Be sharply mindful of any tingling in the stomach, heaviness in the chest, or tightness in the throat. Mindfully attend to such physical experience throughout the contemplation.

5. Note any shifts and conclude with an aspiration. Not all contemplation offers a clear and final resolution, though at times this can be the result. It is likely, however, that our view of life may change during our moment of reflection. Where once there was anger, hesitation, or resistance, there may now be relief, resolve, or sadness. Where once there was longing, there may now be fulfillment, joy, or further curiosity. Such a shift in view or feeling may

inspire us to conduct ourselves differently. You may choose to end the contemplation by writing down an intention. It could be any new behavior or course of action you intend to take because of the contemplation. By ending our contemplation in this way, we can aspire to a fresh perspective and experiment with resourceful ways of being in the world.

APPENDIX F

Suggested Locations for Meditation Retreats

Gampo Abbey
Pleasant Bay
Cape Breton, NS B0E 2P0 Canada
Tel. (902) 224-2752
E-mail: office@gampoabbey.org
Web: www.gampoabbey.org

Green Gulch Farm
1601 Shoreline Highway
Muir Beach, CA 94965
Tel. (415) 383-3134
E-mail: ggfoffice@sfzc.org
Web: www.sfzc.org

Karma Triyana Dharmachakra
335 Meads Mountain Road
Woodstock, NY 12498
Tel. (845) 679-5906 ext. 3
E-mail: office@kagyu.org
Web: www.kagyu.org

Karmê Chöling
369 Patneaude Lane
Barnet, VT 05821
Tel. (802) 633-2384
E-mail: reception@karmecholing.org
Web: www.karmecholing.org

Shambhala Mountain Center
151 Shambhala Way
Red Feather Lakes, CO 80545
Tel. (970) 881-2184
E-mail: callcenter@shambhalamountain.org
Web: www.shambhalamountain.org

Zen Mountain Monastery
P.O. Box 197
Mt. Tremper, NY 12457
Tel. (845) 688-2228
E-mail: zmmtrain@mro.org
Web: www.mro.org

NOTES

Introduction

1. Michael Carroll, *Awake at Work* (Boston: Shambhala Publications, 2004), chap. 17.
2. Michael Carroll, *The Mindful Leader* (Boston: Shambhala Publications, 2007), chap. 21.
3. Chögyam Trungpa, *Shambhala: The Sacred Path of the Warrior* (Boston: Shambhala Publications, 2009), 28.

Chapter 1. *Face the fierce facts of life*

1. World Health Organization Fact Sheet No. 297, February 2009.
2. Rasmussen Reports, August 10, 2010.
3. David Orr, "What Is Education For?" *In Context* 27 (Winter 1991): 52.
4. Anup Shah, ed., www.globalissues.org/article/26/poverty-facts-and-stats.

5. Matthew White, "Historical Atlas of the Twentieth Century," http://users.erols.com/mwhite28/20centry.htm.

Chapter 3. *Recognize fear*

1. *Timuk* in Tibetan, meaning a form of panic marked by being disoriented and dumbfounded.

Chapter 6. *Stop the "bubble wrap"*

1. Fiona Lee, "Fear Factor," *Harvard Business Review* (January 2001).

Chapter 8. *Break the false promise*

1. From "Beauty and the Beast of Advertising," *Media and Values*, no. 49 (Winter 1990).
2. Roxanne Dryden-Edwards, MD, "Anorexia Nervosa," www.medicinenet.com/anorexia_nervosa/article.htm.
3. "Beauty and the Beast of Advertising."

Chapter 14. *Lean in*

1. Carroll, *Awake at Work*, 170–73.
2. Carroll, *The Mindful Leader*, 106–14.

Chapter 15. *Keep your feet on the ground*

1. Matthew Killingsworth et al., "A Wandering Mind Is an Unhappy Mind," *Science* 330, no. 6006 (November 12, 2010).
2. Ibid., 932.
3. Matthew Killingsworth, "The Future of Happiness Research," *Harvard Business Review* (January–February 2012): 89.

Chapter 16. *Stabilize attention*

1. John Freeman, "Manifesto for Slow Communications," *Wall Street Journal*, August 21, 2009.
2. Ibid.

Chapter 17. *Synchronize with the present moment*

1. Trungpa, *Shambhala*, 53.

Chapter 18. *See clearly*

1. Jeff Weiss, Aram Donigan, and Jonathan Hughes, "Extreme Negotiations," *Harvard Business Review* 88, no. 11 (November 2010): 66–75.

Chapter 19. *Don't shortchange yourself*

1. Khenchen Thrangu, *Shenpen Ösel* 4, no. 3 (December 2000): 39. See also Khenchen Thrangu, *Pointing Out the Dharmakaya* (Ithaca, N.Y.: Snow Lion Publications, 2003).
2. Chögyam Trungpa, *Smile at Fear: Awakening the True Heart of Bravery* (Boston: Shambhala Publications, 2010), 111.

Chapter 20. *Be vividly present*

1. Li Huang, Adam D. Galinsky, Deborah H. Gruenfeld, and Lucia E. Guillory, "Powerful Postures versus Powerful Roles: Which Is the Proximate Correlate of Thought and Behavior?" *Psychological Science* (December 2010).
2. Chögyam Trungpa, *Great Eastern Sun: The Wisdom of Shambhala* (Boston: Shambhala Publications, 2001), 178.

Chapter 22. *Be, see, do*

1. Peter Haskel, *Bankei Zen* (New York: Grove Press, 1984), 4.
2. Ibid, 87.
3. Richard Pascale, Jerry Sternin, and Monique Sternin, *The Power of Positive Deviance* (Boston: Harvard Business Publishing, 2010).

Chapter 24. *Where's the edge?*

1. Harvey Hornstein, *Managerial Courage* (New York: Wiley, 1986), 98–102.
2. Bruce Tuckman, "Developmental Sequence in Small Groups," *Psychological Bulletin* 63, no. 6 (1965): 384–99.

Chapter 25. *Take a straight dose*

1. Salle Tisdale, "Washing Out Emptiness," *Tricycle* 17 (Fall 2007).

Chapter 26. *Be a spiritual fool*

1. Chögyam Trungpa, *Wise Fool*, in *The Collected Works of Chögyam Trungpa*, vol. 7 (Boston: Shambhala Publications, 2003), 107.

Chapter 27. *Hold sadness and joy*

1. Mother Teresa, 1979 Nobel Peace Prize lecture, www.nobelprize.org.
2. Chögyam Trungpa, "Conquering Fear," in *The Collected Works of Chögyam Trungpa*, vol. 8 (Boston: Shambhala Publications, 2004), 396.

Chapter 30. *Gently bow*

1. Hakuyu Taizan Maezumi and Bernard Tetsugen Glassman, eds., in "Notes on Gassho and Bowing," *On Zen Practice* (Boulder, Colo.: Great Eastern Book Co., 1977), 54–61; reprinted in *Gassho* 1, no. 1 (November 1993).
2. www.worldometers.info.
3. www.fao.org/forestry/fra/en.
4. www.who.int/tobacco/en/atlas8.pdf.
5. www.infurmation.com/about.php.
6. Carroll, *Awake at Work*, 89–91.

Chapter 31. *In a word*

1. Bennett Miller, director, *Moneyball* (Sony Pictures, 2011).

Chapter 32. *Join heaven and earth*

1. Chögyam Trungpa, *True Command: The Teachings of the Dorje Kasung* (Halifax, Nova Scotia: Trident Publications, 2003).
2. Longchenpa, *Old Man Basking in the Sun: Longchenpa's Treasury of Natural Perfection*, trans. Keith Dowman (Kathmandu, Nepal: Vajra Publications, 2007).
3. Chögyam Trungpa, *The Collected Works of Chögyam Trungpa*, vol. 1 (Boston: Shambhala Publications, 2004), 461.
4. Dudjom Rinpoche, *Counsels from My Heart* (Boston: Shambhala Publications, 2001), 85.
5. Dilgo Khyentse, *Primordial Purity* (Halifax, Nova Scotia: Vajravairochana Translation Committee, 1999), 47.

Chapter 35. *Unseen precise hand*

1. Carroll, *Awake at Work*, 130–34.

Chapter 36. *Just slow down*

1. "The American Freshman: National Norms Fall 2010," *New York Times*, January 26, 2011.
2. Vicki Abeles, producer and codirector, *Race to Nowhere* (Reel Link Films, 2009).
3. www.suicide.org.
4. In business terminology, *silos* are aligned yet isolated and uncoordinated functions.
5. http://en.wikipedia.org/wiki/Slow_movement.

Chapter 38. *Resonate*

1. Daniel Goleman, *Social Intelligence: The Revolutionary New Science of Human Relationships* (New York: Bantam Books, 2006), 4.
2. Daniel Stern, *The Present Moment in Psychotherapy and Everyday Life* (New York: Norton, 2004), 76.
3. Ibid.
4. Jeffrey Cohn, Jon Katzenbach, and Gus Vlak, "Finding and Grooming Breakthrough Innovators," *Harvard Business Review* (December 2008).

Appendix A. *Cultivating Fearlessness through* Shiné-Lhagtong *Meditation*

1. Yi Yuan Tang, MD, PhD, "Integrative Body Mind Training (IBMT) Meditation Found to Boost Brain Connectivity," *Science Daily* 107, no. 35 (August 18, 2010).

2. Davidson et al., "Alterations in Brain and Immune Function Produced by Mindfulness Meditation," *Psychosomatic Medicine* 65 (2003): 564–70.

3. Kirk Warren Brown and Richard M. Ryan, "The Benefits of Being Present: Mindfulness and Its Role in Psychological Well-Being," *Journal of Personality and Social Psychology* 84, vol. 4 (April 2003): 822–48.

4. Carroll, *The Mindful Leader*, 13–30.

5. Traleg Kyabgon, *Mind at Ease* (Boston: Shambhala Publications, 2004); Dakpo Tashi Namgyal, *Clarifying the Natural State* (Kathmandu, Nepal: Rangjung Yeshe Publications, 2001); and Khenchen Thrangu Rinpoche, *Crystal Clear* (Kathmandu, Nepal: Ranjung Yeshe Publications, 2003).

6. Herbert Guenther, *The Life and Teaching of Naropa* (New York: Oxford University Press, 1963).

7. Peter Haskel, *Bankei Zen* (New York: Grove Press), 1984.

8. http://en.wikipedia.org/wiki/Mahakasyapa.

Appendix C. *How Mindfulness-Awareness Cultivates Social Intelligence*

1. Goleman, *Social Intelligence*, 84.

2. Ibid., 85.

3. Ibid., 84.

4. Ibid., 86.

5. Carroll, *The Mindful Leader*, chaps. 7 and 8.

6. Goleman, *Social Intelligence*, 84.

7. Ibid., 89.

8. Ibid., 84.

9. Ibid., 89.
10. Ibid., 84.
11. Ibid., 91.
12. Ibid., 84.
13. Ibid., 94.
14. Carroll, *The Mindful Leader*, chap. 5.
15. Goleman, *Social Intelligence*, 84.
16. Ibid., 95.
17. Carroll, *The Mindful Leader*, chap. 13.
18. Goleman, *Social Intelligence*, 84.
19. Ibid., 96.
20. Carroll, *Awake at Work*, chap. 3; and Carroll, *The Mindful Leader*, chap. 1.

Appendix D: *Four Fearless Traditions*

1. Chögyam Trungpa Rinpoche was a meditation master of both the Kagyu and Nyingma lineages of Tibetan Buddhism. Born into the Mukpo clan of Tibet, he was recognized as the eleventh Trungpa Tulku at an early age and was enthroned while a child as the supreme abbot of the Surmang monasteries. A *tertön* (or discoverer of secret teachings), scholar, teacher, poet, and founder of Shambhala Training, Trungpa Rinpoche died at the age of forty-eight on April 4, 1987.

2. The Sixteenth Karmapa, Rangjung Rigpe Dorje, was the supreme head of the Kagyu lineage of Tibetan Buddhism. Born in Kham in eastern Tibet in August 1924, he was recognized and enthroned as the Karmapa at an early age and remained the Kagyu spiritual leader until his death on November 5,

1981. A scholar, teacher, and ornithologist extraordinaire, Rangjung Rigpe Dorje's mere presence as a Buddhist king was renowned for inspiring profound and lasting human transformation.

3. His Holiness Dilgo Khyentse Rinpoche was the supreme head of the Nyingma lineage of Tibetan Buddhism from 1987 until his death on September 28, 1991. Born in the Denhok Valley of Kham in eastern Tibet in 1910, he was recognized at the age of seven as one of the incarnations of Jamyang Khyentse Rinpoche. A tertön, scholar, and extraordinary teacher, Dilgo Khyentse Rinpoche was widely considered by all Tibetan schools of Buddhism as the preeminent realized teacher of his time.

4. Trungpa, *Shambhala*, 25–27.

5. Sun Tzu, *The Art of War: The Denma Translation*, trans. Denma Translation Group (Boston: Shambhala Publications, 2002).

6. Carroll, *Awake at Work*, 114.

7. Erik Pema Kunsang and Marcia Binder Schmidt, eds., *Blazing Splendor: The Memoirs of Tulku Urgyen Rinpoche* (Kathmandu, Nepal: Rangjung Yeshe Publications, 2005), 29 and 377.

ABOUT THE AUTHOR

Over his thirty-year business career, Michael Carroll has held executive positions with such companies as Shearson Lehman/ American Express, Simon & Schuster, and the Walt Disney Company, and today he has an active consulting, training, and coaching business with many client firms, such as Procter & Gamble, Google, AstraZeneca, Starbucks, National Geographic Expeditions, and Merck.

Michael has been studying Tibetan Buddhism since 1976, graduated from Buddhist seminary in 1980, and is an authorized teacher in the Kagyu-Nyingma and Shambhala lineages of Tibetan Buddhism. Michael received his bachelor's degree in theology and philosophy from the University of Dayton and his master's degree in adult education from Hunter College and has lectured and taught at Wharton Business School, Columbia University, Swarthmore College, Yale University, University of Sydney, St. Mary's University, University of Toronto, Drexel University, Virginia Tech, Kripalu, Cape Cod Institute, Zen Mountain Monastery, Shambhala Mountain Center, Karme Chöling, Evam

Institute, Omega Institute (assisting Pema Chödrön), and many other practice centers throughout the United States, Canada, Europe, and Australia.